SOLOMON & SHEBA

The Queen of Sheba arrives at Solomon's palace in Jerusalem. This is a stained glass roundel from the north side of the Canterbury Cathedral. (Late 20th century, from the Victoria and Albert Museum, London.)

SOLOMON & SHEBA

INNER MARRIAGE AND INDIVIDUATION

Barbara Black Koltuv, Ph.D.

Nicolas-Hays, Inc.
York Beach, Maine

First published in 1993 by
Nicolas-Hays, Inc.
Box 612
York Beach, ME 03910

Distributed to the trade by
Samuel Weiser, Inc.
Box 612
York Beach, ME 03910

Library of Congress Cataloging-in-Publication Data

Koltuv, Barbara Black.
    Solomon and Sheba / by Barbara Black Koltuv.
        p.   cm.
    Includes index.
    1. Solomon, King of Israel--Legends.   2. Sheba, Queen
of--Legends.   I. Title.
    BS580.S6K63   1993
    222'.530922--dc20   92-44082
                                                                    CIP
ISBN 0-89254-024-9
BJ

Cover art is titled *Solomon and Sheba* by Duncan Grant (1885–
1978). Copyright © 1993 Artist's estate. Used by kind permission
of The Bridgeman Art Library, London.

Typeset in 11 point Palatino

Printed in the United States of America

The paper used in this publication meets the minimum requirements of the American National Standard for Permanence of
Paper for Printed Library Materials Z39.48–1984.

For Stan,
and for
Abdul Jami, his teachers, and mine.

Table of Contents

Introduction ix

Chapter 1. The Realm of Solomon 1

Chapter 2. The Land of Sheba 17

Chapter 3. The Need—The Call 35

Chapter 4. The Testing of Hearts 63

Chapter 5. Riddle Me This, Riddle Me That 81

Chapter 6. The Coniunctio—The Knowing
             Connection 89

Chapter 7. King Solomon's Decline 111

Chapter 8. The Song of Aurora Dawn 123

Epilogue 137

Bibliography 139

About the author 141

Introduction

The ancient stories, dreams and images always stay with me, in my heart, particularly the love stories: Jacob and Rachel, David and Bathsheba, and most of all Solomon and Sheba. This tale of King and Queen, he and she, lovers, meeting, testing, knowing, connecting, and parting, has been given and received in both the Old and New Testaments, in the Qur'an, and in the Holy Book of the Coptic Ethiopian Orthodox Church, the *Kebra Nagast*, or *The Book of the Glory of Kings*. There, it is told as the story of the Queen of Sheba and her only son Menyelek, whose father is Solomon. It is said that the word of God was dictated and written into these holy books in the daytime, but that the interpretations were given and are given at night in dreams, and they are told by storytellers the world over, forever. The Sufis say a dream is one fortieth prophecy . . .

I am going to deal with the story of Solomon and Sheba as though it is all one story. I will give bibliographic references to the original recorded texts and preserved tablets telling of certain elements of the myth, but I will tell the story as I believe it to be true. I have become my own storyteller. None of it is original. All of it is.

The story, or the archetype of Solomon and Sheba, may be understood on several levels. It is a simple, splendid love story of a wise and wealthy King, visited by a beautiful, exotic Queen. They meet, she opens her heart to him and he gives her all that she asks of him, and then they part. It is also the story of the heart's journey toward individuation and inner marriage, a *con-*

iunctio of the masculine and feminine principles existing in every human psyche resulting in a new birth, and it is unmistakably a story of mystical love, the love of God.

And Ezra the scribe stood upon a dais of wood, which they had made for the purpose; and beside him stood the other scribes, story-tellers, and singers. . . . And Ezra opened the Book in the sight of all the people—for he was above all the people—and he read from the Book. And the story-tellers and even the priests and teachers caused the people to understand the Book of the Laws; and the people stood in their place. And they, the story-tellers and teachers and scribes, read in the Book, in the Law of God, distinctly; and they gave the sense, and caused all the people to understand the reading (Nehemiah 8:4–9).

For it *is*, always *is*, however much we say it was. Thus speaks the myth, which is only the garment of the mystery (Thomas Mann, *Joseph and His Brothers*, Knopf: New York, 1963, p. 33).

Feast of story-telling, thou art the festal garment of life's mystery (*Ibid*).

God made man because he loves stories (Elie Weisel, *Gates to the Forest*).

Chapter 1

THE REALM OF SOLOMON

Now, once upon a time, when King David was old and stricken in years, they covered him with robes and quilts but he could get no warmth. So they sought a fair young virgin to be a companion to him and lie with him so that the King could get warmth. Though the comely young woman from Shunam, Abishag, did become a companion to him and minister to him, David's fire was not rekindled and he was unable to know her carnally. His son Adonijah, sensing his father's demise, exalted himself, saying, "I will be king." Nathan the prophet warned Bathsheba, the Queen, of Adonijah's attempt to usurp David's throne, and reminded her that David had indeed sworn to her that their son, Solomon, David's only love child, would reign after him. Bathsheba went into the King's chamber. He was very old and Abishag the Shunamite maiden ministered to him, and Bath-sheba bowed and prostrated herself before him, and reminded him that he had sworn to her before God that their son Solomon would reign after David. And Nathan the prophet also came before David and told him of Adonijah's plans and asked, "Is this what you want?" Thereupon King David called Bathsheba into his presence and said:

> As the Lord liveth, who hath redeemed my soul out of all adversity, verily as I swore unto thee by the Lord, the God of Israel saying: Assuredly Solomon thy son shall reign after me, and he shall sit upon my throne in my stead; verily so will I do this day. Then Bathsheba bowed with her face to the earth, and prostrated herself to the King, and said: "Let my Lord King David live forever" (I Kings 1:1–32).

When David slept with his fathers in the city of David on the hillside of Ur-Salim, Jerusalem, city of peace, his son Solomon became king. Solomon had killed or exiled his enemies, and the enemies of his father David, and established himself on the throne. He allied himself with Pharaoh, King of Egypt, by marriage to the pharaoh's daughter and took her to live with him in the city of David (I Kings 2:10–3:4).

Although Solomon loved the Lord and walked in the statutes of David, his father, he continued to offer sacrifice in the high places to other gods. At Gibeon, a great high place where Solomon had offered a thousand burnt offerings upon the altar, God appeared to him in a dream one night and said, "Ask what I shall give thee." Solomon replied that God had given his father, David, great kindness and the ability to walk before God in truth and righteousness with an upright heart, but that he, Solomon, felt that compared with his father, "I am but a little child; I know not how to go out or come in." He continued saying to God that as king he needed an understanding heart—literally, a listening heart—so that he could judge people and discern between good and evil (I Kings 3:2–10).

Because Solomon had asked nothing for himself, not a long life, nor riches, nor the lives of his enemies, God said, "Lo, I will give thee an wise and understanding heart, like none before or after thee." And God added that He would also give what Solomon had not asked—both riches and honor—and if Solomon walked in the way of God, and kept his commandments, He would also give him a long life. Solomon awoke and beheld it was a dream; and he came back to Jerusalem and stood before the ark of the covenant of the Lord and offered up burnt offerings, and offered peace offerings, and made a feast for all of his people (I Kings 3:12–16).

Soon afterward the two women who were harlots who had each given birth the same night in the same house appeared before King Solomon. One baby had died in the night, and both women claimed the living child as her own. Solomon said, "Fetch me a sword," and then he said, "Divide the living child in two and give half to one and half to the other." The true mother said, "Oh no, give *her* the living child, do not kill it," but the other said, "Yes, divide it." All Israel heard of Solomon's judgment and saw that the wisdom of God was in him to do justice (I Kings 3:16–28).

So Solomon reigned in a time of peace and prosperity. He had twelve officers, all stationed in a different part of his land. They each provided the victuals for the King and his household for one month of the year. Solomon had an entire city devoted to the making of arms. The Old Testament describes the richness and abundance of Solomon's realm: nothing was lacking and Solomon's wisdom surpassed the wisdom of the East and the wisdom of Egypt, and Solomon spoke three thousand proverbs and wrote a thousand and five songs (I Kings 5–13).

The Qur'an, too, tells of Solomon's procreativity and lists him among the founders of families (S VI 84). It carefully notes that he could distinguish good from evil (S II 102), and was wise in that he had right understanding and discernment (S XXXI 79), citing an incident that occurred when Solomon was only 11 years old and David (his father) was still king: on account of the negligence of the shepherd some sheep got into a cultivated field or vineyard by night and ate up all the young plants and their tender shoots. David considered the matter to be so serious that he awarded the owner of the field the sheep themselves in compensation for this damage. Solomon, though only a boy, thought of a more differentiated solution where the penalty better suited the offense. Solomon's suggestion was that since the loss was the loss of the fruits or produce of the field while the *corpus* of the property was not lost, the owner of the field should not take the sheep altogether, but should instead only detain them long enough to recoup his actual damage from the milk, wool, and possibly the young of the sheep, and then return the flock to the shepherd.

Solomon's wisdom extended to the natural sciences as well, and is extolled in both the Bible and Qur'an. He spoke of trees, from the cedar that is in Lebanon to the common hyssop that grows out of a wall. He spoke also of beasts, and of fowl, and of creeping things and of fishes (I Kings 13). The Qur'an continues, He was well versed in knowledge and mystic wisdom (S XXVII 14–15). He could understand the wisdom of the humble ant and the Speech of Birds (S XXVII 16). God made even the unruly wind blow tamely for Solomon (S XXI 81) so that a month's journey by land could be accomplished in a morning or an evening at sea (S XXXIV 12). The Bible also notes Solomon's navy, but says its success stemmed from Hiram's gift to Solomon of accomplished, knowledgeable seamen, who sailed from Exion-Geber to Ophir and returned with gold for Solomon (I Kings 25–26). One may read in the Qur'an that even the very land was subject to Solomon's desire in that huge stones could be cut to his order (S XXI 81). The evil ones, or djinns, worked for Solomon by leave of Allah in that Solomon tamed evil with wisdom. See figure 1, page 6. If any of them refused, they tasted the Penalty of Blazing fire (S XXXIV 12). The djinns rebuilt palaces, made statues, gardens, ponds and precious carpets for Solomon. When he desired to travel they carried him on their backs. (See figure 2, p. 8.)

One of the tasks done by the djinns was to dive beneath the sea to secure pearls and other treasure for Solomon (S XXI 82). And they did other work for him as well: God made a font of molten brass flow for Solomon, and the djinns worked it for him as he desired,

Figure 1. Solomon commanding the djinns (from the British Library, Or MS 4383 Folio 143v).

making arches, images, basins as large as reservoirs, and cooking cauldrons (S XXXIV 12–13). Qabalists say that since the Hebrew word for brass contains the word "serpent" (*Nahash*), he had been given serpent power wisdom as well. The Qur'an adds that Solomon was able to marshall all the people, djinns, birds, and forms of knowledge at his disposal and keep them in due order and cooperation (S XXVII 17) so that he could always obtain the best possible results.

Solomon, or Suleiman ibn Daoud as he is called by the Asiatics, is remembered in Arabic, Turkish, and Persian literature, as well. Not only is he the richest and wisest monarch on earth, but his knowledge makes him the most powerful of men. He commands all celestial, terrestrial, and infernal spirits. He is obeyed by the subterranean pygmies and gnomes, and by undines, elves and salamanders.

Islamic philosophers see each of the prophets – Moses, David and Jesus – as a particular channel for the transmission of the divine spirit which initiates, enlivens, and determines. Solomon is seen as having the special spiritual power to master and direct the way physical and elemental things behave. Even Muhammad, who was also granted this power, did not exercise it outwardly as Solomon did. According to the Qur'an, Solomon knew that this dominion was granted him by God the Compassionate and God the Merciful. As the Compassionate, God gives freely, while as the Merciful, He binds by obligation. Solomon's gnosis of God is implicit in his extraordinary accomplishments and use of his gifts.

Solomon was the embodiment of wisdom. Jewish folklore says that he possessed the *shomir*, sometimes described as a worm the size of a grain of wheat, that had the power to cut down huge trees and split mountains into slabs of stone. It is said that the *shomir* was kept in wool in the garden of Eden until Solomon began to build the House of God. Then an eagle was sent to carry it to the builders.

Another legend says the *shomir* was a blue stone, the size of a small jewel. This stone is sometimes likened to the Lapis of the Philosopher's Stone. When it was placed with the intention to break a rock, and the Ineffable name was whispered, the rock beneath would

Figure 2. Solomon's throne borne aloft by his djinns (from British Library, Or MS 5599, Folio 134v).

break into the desired shape and size. Only Asmodeus, King of the Demons who lived in the Mountains of Darkness, knew the hiding place. Solomon was able to extract this secret from Asmodeus by trickery, but when the Temple was completed, the *shomir* was given back to the Keeper of the Abyss who buried it in the Bottomless Sea. None but the Creator himself can extract it from there.

Thus, whether Solomon's wisdom took the form of a tiny primitive life form, a worm, or an essentially hard cutting stone, he could use it to differentiate and shape matter into creative and useful accomplishments.

The Bible tells that in the fourth year of his reign over Israel, shortly after the dream in which he said, "I am but a little child; I know not how to go out or come in," Solomon began to build the house of the Lord (I Kings 6:2). Solomon used the wisdom he had been given to order, administrate, and build. The Kebra Nagast (xlvii), the Holy Book of Ethiopian Coptics, tells of Solomon's abiding personal connection to God while building the temple:

> Solomon the king gave the command that the stones for the building should be hewn in immense sizes. But the workmen were unable to hew such large blocks of stone, and their tools broke when they attempted the work, and they cried out to Solomon the King and besought him to think out in his wisdom some way of lightening their labor. And Solomon entreated God, the bestower of wisdom, to suggest some means to him. And behold, Solomon summoned the hunters and commanded them

to bring a young Rukh bird to the palace and to put over it a brass pot with a space inside it sufficiently large to contain the Rukh bird. The pot had three legs, each one cubit in height, and it stood above the ground, so that the wings of the young bird protruded from under the aforementioned pot. Now, when the mother of the Rukh bird returned to her nest in the high mountains and did not find her young one there, she was disturbed and she flew round and round over the earth seeking for it. And she flew over Jerusalem and saw her young one there, but had not the power to seize it. She mounted up into the heights and went toward the paradise of God, in the Eastern part of Eden, and she found below paradise a piece of wood which had been cast down there as if for her to carry it away. She seized it, and by reason of her great sorrow for her young one she took not rest until she had brought it to Jerusalem, and hurled it down upon the brass pot. By the might of God a miracle took place forthwith: the pot split into two halves, and the mother Rukh saw her young one, and caught it up, and bore it off to her nest. When Solomon and all the children of Israel saw this miracle, with a loud voice they praised the Almighty, the Governor of the Universe, Who had bestowed upon a bird that was not endowed with reasoning powers the instinct to do that which human beings could not do. Straightaway King Solomon commanded the stone masons to take that piece of holy and blessed wood, and when they had

marked out and measured the stone which they
wished to split, to lay the aforementioned piece
of wood on the place marked. When they had
done this, by the might of God the stone split
wheresoever they wished it to split, and they
found their work easy.

Because of this very strong sign from God, Solomon
became certain in his own mind that the Governor of
the Universe regarded the building of the Temple with
favor. When the construction of the temple was finished, the aforementioned piece of wood was placed in
the entrance chamber of the forecourt of the Holy Temple and held in respect. Its operative power in building
the temple had come to an end, but its role in the story
of Solomon and Sheba continued, as we shall see.

Solomon did build a house of stone for the Lord. It
is described fully in the Old Testament (I Kings 6:2–37).
(See figure 3 on page 12.) He covered the stone with
carved cedar wood. In the innermost part of the house
there was a sanctuary for the ark of the covenant overlaid with pure gold. He placed an altar of cedar before
the ark. Then he covered the entire house inside with
pure gold and drew chains of gold across the wall
before the sanctuary and overlaid it with gold. The
whole house he overlaid with gold, until all the house
was finished; also the whole altar that belonged to the
sanctuary he overlaid with gold. . . . And in the sanctuary he made two cherubim of olive wood, and the
wings of the cherubim stretched from one wall to the
other of the inner chamber, and he overlaid the cherubim with gold. And he carved all the walls with cherubim, and palm trees, and open flowers within and with-

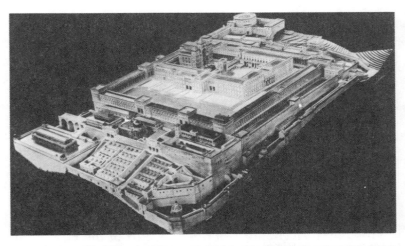

Figure 3. A) Model of Solomon's Temple at Jerusalem (from the Mansell Collection, London); B) Another attempt to reconstruct the Jerusalem Temple (from *Biblical Archaeologist:* Harvard University, G. E. Wright and F. Albright, cited in *Solomon and Sheba,* edited by J. B. Pritchard, London, Phaidon Press, 1981).

out, and the floor of the house he overlaid with gold within and without, and the inner doors and outer doors were all carved and overlaid with pure gold. In eleven years the house of the Lord was completed.

Solomon also built a house for himself called The Forest of Lebanon. It was a hundred cubits long, fifty broad, and thirty high, with ceilings of cedar wood and a multitude of columns. He built another like it for the daughter of the Pharaoh. He fetched Hiram of Tyre to work in brass, because Hiram was filled with wisdom and understanding and skill to work in all things of brass. Hiram fashioned huge pillars topped with nets of checkerwork, wreaths of chain work, lilies, and a row of some two hundred pomegranates. The right pillar was called Joachim and the left Boas. Then Solomon had Hiram make a molten sea of brass, six cubits from drain to drain, and five cubits high. It was surrounded by two rows of knobs. It stood upon twelve oxen, three looking toward the north, three looking toward the west, three looking toward the south and three looking toward the east. It was a hand's breadth thick, and the lip was wrought like a cup, like the flower of a lily, and it held two thousand baths. He made ten basins of brass and a border with lions, oxen, cherubim, and palm trees. Every basin had wheels and axles also of brass and contained forty baths. Solomon left all the vessels unweighed because they were exceedingly many and the weight of the brass could not be found out.

Solomon made all the vessels that were to be in the house of the Lord of gold. The altar, the table where the showbread was, the candlesticks, five on the left and five on the right of the sanctuary, the flowers, the lamps, the tongs, cups, snuffers, basins, pans, fire pans and all the hinges for both the inner sanctuary doors and the doors to the house were all of pure gold.

The twenty years of elaborate building included the Temple, the king's house, the house of the daughter of Pharaoh, Millo, the wall around Jerusalem, Hazor, Megiddo, and Gezer, Beth-horon, Baalath and Tadmor in the wilderness, plus store-cities, and places for his horses and chariots and horsemen.

Solomon lived in luxury. Even his targets and shields were made of beaten gold. His throne was ivory overlaid with the finest gold. There were six steps to the throne. It was round behind and there were armrests on either side of the seat with a lion standing beside each arm. Twelve lions stood on either side of the six steps. There was not the like of it made in any other kingdom.

All the drinking cups and vessels in King Solomon's house were of pure gold; none were of silver. Nothing was accounted for in the days of Solomon, for the king had the navy of Tarshish and the navy of Hiram bringing him every three years gold and silver, ivory, and apes and peacocks (I Kings 6:10–23).

Both Holy Books, the Bible and Qur'an, emphasize the wealth and wisdom and glory of the age of Solomon. However both note the points of trouble, too. The Bible says that Solomon used forced labor, slavery and heavy taxation to accomplish his extensive building program. Solomon's despotism is clearly apparent in this statement of his son, Rehoboam, "My father made your yoke heavy, but I will add to your yoke; my father chastised you with whips, but I will chastise you with scorpions (I Kings 12:14).

In the realm of religious practice, the Old Testament is even more seriously critical of Solomon. He did what was evil in the sight of the Lord: he loved many foreign women besides the daughter of Pharoah—Moabites, Ammonites, Edomites, Zidonians and Hittites—and they turned his heart away from the Lord to their own gods. And he worshipped the goddess Ashtoreth and the detestations Milcom, Molech, and Chemosh, and built altars for them in high places in order to worship these idols. I Kings 10:14 states that in one year Solomon received 666 talents of gold. This number is the mystic number of the triple Goddess and was later interpreted in the New Testament as the number of the beast (Revelation 13:18) and is further evidence of Solomon's yearning toward Goddess worship.

The Qur'an hints at criticism of Solomon for practicing occult arts, and for dalliance with the supernatural, but says specifically, that while some of the People of the Book threw away their own Book of God and followed what the evil ones gave out (falsely) against the power of Solomon, the blasphemers were *not Solomon* (italics mine), but the evil ones teaching men magic and such things (S II 101–103).

Oriental folklore holds that Solomon's seal, his mysterious lamp, his throne, and above all, his ring, were endowed with magical powers. One day, he is said to have assembled all the djinns and impressed the seal of his ring upon their necks to mark them as his slaves. Then, while bathing in the Jordan, Solomon lost the ring and was without knowledge and wisdom until a fisherman, who had found it inside a fish, brought it back to him. It is also believed by some, that on this occasion Solomon was robbed of his ring by a jealous djinn. The djinn seated himself on the throne and reigned in Solomon's place, while the deposed Solomon became a wanderer until the moment when the djinn, compelled by God, threw the ring into the sea.

Thus, while folklore accounts for certain lapses into despotism and idolatry on Solomon's part, by saying that he was robbed, he was not himself, and so on, these tales do bespeak an opening, a wound or need in the otherwise powerful glory and wisdom of the King, Solomon.

Psychologically, Solomon may be seen as a kind of highly developed form of ego functioning. Knowledge, understanding, discernment and effectiveness are highly valued motives. Overwork and overreach are common among people who, like Solomon, serve ego as King. However, like Solomon, ego-ridden people also suffer a sense of loss, a yearning for something more.

Chapter 2

THE LAND
OF SHEBA

Solomon, son of David, was king of the Hebrews. His palace was in Jerusalem and his realm extended from the Euphrates to the land of the Philistines and to the borders of Egypt (I Kings 5:1). He is forever fixed in place as the wise and wealthy king who was visited by the Queen of Sheba.

"Who do you think you are, the Queen of Sheba?" These two questions, often asked, raise several others. Who *is* the Queen of Sheba? She has many names. Queen of the South to the Christians (Matthew 12:42; Luke 11:31). Makeda to the Ethiopian Coptics (Kebra Nagast), Balqis to the Arabs (Qur'an S XXVII and XXXIV), and Candace and Nikaule to the ancient Greeks and Romans. The alchemists call the Queen of Sheba Aurora Dawn (consurgens) and the *sal sapientae*, the pure, chaste, white dove wherein is the magistery of

Figure 4. The Queen of Sheba wearing regal robes. (Ms. Rome, Biblioteca Apostolica Vaticana. Cod: Urb. lat. 899. Nicolò d'Antonio degli Agli, *Le Nozze di Costanzo Sforza e Camilla d'Aragona,* fol. 88r.)

the work. Josephus, the Jewish historian, avoids the issue of her name altogether, and calls her the Queen of Egypt and Ethiopia (*Antiquities*, Book VIII, 6. 5–6). See figure 4 on page 18.

While Hiram of Tyre is often mentioned in the Old Testament story of Solomon and Sheba both with and without his royal title, the name of the Queen of Sheba is never mentioned. The Queen, however, does refer to having heard of Solomon *in mine own land* (I Kings 10:6) and there are many references to the land and people of Sheba throughout the Old Testament (Genesis 10:7, 25; Psalms 72:10, 15; Isaiah 60:6; Jeremiah 6:20; Ezekiel 27:20ff; Joel 3:8).

Where is the land of Sheba? Arabia Felix, South Arabia, Yemen, Ethiopia, Egypt, Kush and Punt, are all named as her land. Clouds of fantasy and mystery obscure the exact location. Her capital was at Marib near Sa'ana in South Yemen (see figure 5, p. 20). She is called Sheba as is her land and tribe, so much *of* her land is she.

> There lived she years ninety, subduing
>   the land
> from distant Iraq to the edge of sand
> A thousand thousand her orders obey
> Each ready to serve her by night and by day
> > (Ode to the Queen of Sheba
> > by Ab-Karib As'ad,
> > a Sabean king
> > who reigned A.D. 375 to 425.)

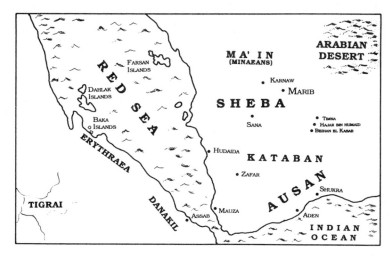

Figure 5. Yemen and Ethiopia and the land of Sheba.
(After Sabatino Moscati, Ancient Semitic Civilizations,
Elec Books, 1957, page 182.)

The land of Sheba itself had been sculpted into
dams and canals. Each year when the flooding mon-
soon rains, called *sur*, came to the dry, parched lands,
instead of running off the top of the earth in sheets, the
sculpted land caught it in pools and cisterns and chan-
nels and distributed it as widely and as quickly as possible. Nowhere were the dams intended to impound the
water. The sluices at either end of the great dam at
Marib could not be closed off. Instead, the natural elements of rain, land, and air were melded to create life,
growth, and nourishment. Sheba's land had been gifted
by God, Allah, as the Queen states in the Sura about
Sheba:

He knows all that goes
into the earth and all that
comes out thereof;
all that comes down from the sky
and all that ascends thereto.
And He is the most Merciful, the All-Forgiving.
(S XXXIV,2)

The people of Sheba's realm knew and understood this aspect of God's gifts to them. So Sheba's land was always green and there was plenty to eat. The Qur'an continues:

There was for Sheba, aforetimes, a Sign in their
Home-land—two gardens—one to the right and
one to the left. "Eat of the sustenance provided
by your Lord, and be grateful to Him: a territory
fair and happy, and a Lord Oft-Forgiving."
(S XXXIV, 15)

Wherever one looked in the land of Sheba on either side of the extensive irrigating canals there was greenery, earning for this Garden of Eden the name Araby Felix, Araby the Blest.

In that region, and in that region only, the trees ran with resins of frankincense and myrrh which the people of Sheba collected. (See figures 6 and 7, pp. 22 and 23.) From the Wise Men's gifts to Jesus (Matthew 2:11) we know that frankincense and myrrh were ranked with gold as gifts suitable for a king. They were used in ritual, as an incense, and as a preservative of bodies. They were used for healing and for beauty treatments, as in the story of Esther in the Old Testament:

It had been done to her according to the law for women, twelve months—for so were the days of their anointing accomplished, to wit, six months with oil of myrrh, and six months with sweet odours, and with other ointments of the women (Esther 2:12).

A great highway of incense routes went from Sheba to Syria and the flourishing Kingdoms of the Euphrates and Tigris valleys on the one hand and Egypt on the other, and with the great Roman Empire around the Mediterranean (see figure 8, page 24). At the other end—through the Yemen coast—the road connected by sea transport with India, Malaya and China (see figure 9 on page 25). No wonder the Qur'an speaks of Sheba as a place upon which Allah had poured his blessings. "Between Sheba and Damascus, Alexandria and Bagh-

Figure 6. Measuring myrrh in the Land of Punt. From Queen Hatshepsut's mortuary temple reliefs at Deir el-Bahri (from *Solomon and Sheba*, edited by J. B. Pritchard, Phaidon Press, London, 1974).

Figure 7. Frankincense "tears" forming on a tapped tree on the spice route (from *Solomon and Sheba,* edited by J. B. Pritchard, Phaidon Press, London, 1974).

dad, we had placed cities in prominent positions: Jerusalem and Media are there for example. And between them We had appointed stages of a journey in their proportion: Travel therein secure, by night and by day." (S XXXIV 18). It is likely that Sheba had negotiated agreements for passage with all the tribes along the incense routes as well as with Solomon, who had control of all terminal ports of the major roads. The Queen of Sheba sent on camels the lightest and most valuable crop—incense of frankincense and myrrh, and the camels returned bearing gold. (See figure 10, page 26.) The

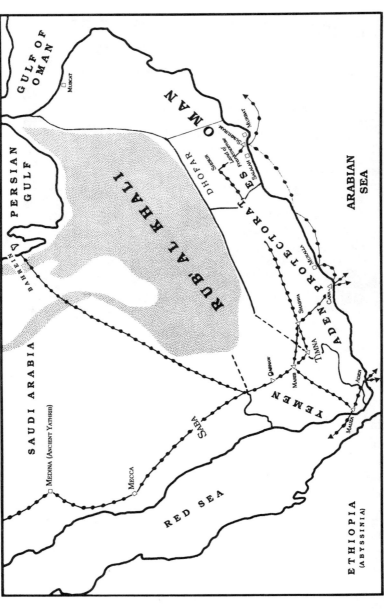

Figure 8. Incense and spice routes in Ethiopia (Abyssinia). (After Wendell Phillips, *Qataban and Sheba*, Harcourt Brace, New York, 1955.)

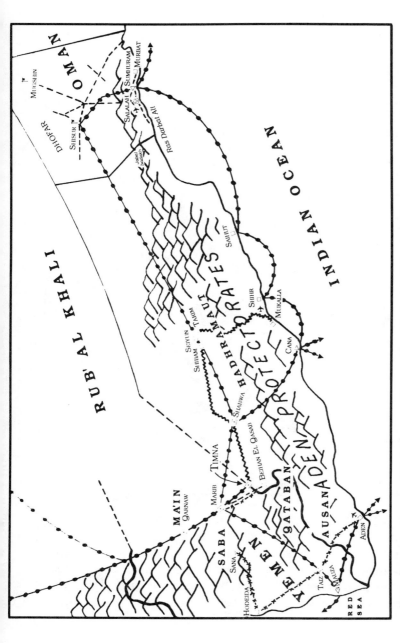

Figure 9. Yemen and Saba were the source of the ancient incense routes to India, Maylaya, and China. Saba is another name for Sheba. (After Wendell Phillips, Qataban and Sheba, Harcourt Brace, New York, 1955.)

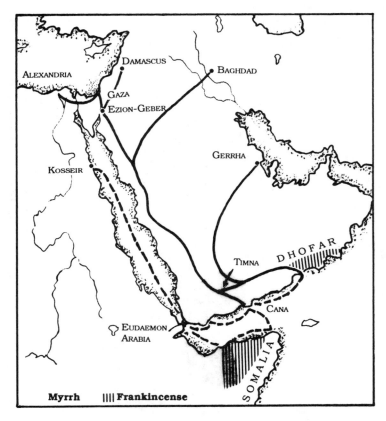

Figure 10. A sketch that shows the approximate zones where frankincense and myrrh are grown in southern Arabia and northern Somalia. Also indicated are major incense routes, by both land and sea, that developed in order to distribute these substances. (Adapted from J. B. Pritchard, *Solomon and Sheba*, Phaidon Press, London, 1974.)

Figure 11. The multitude of camels and dromedaries from Sheba shall come.

gold stayed in Sheba's land. They had no need to purchase anything, being agriculturally self-sufficient in their irrigated splendor. As Isaiah (60:6) puts it: "The multitude of camels shall cover thee, the dromedaries of Midian and Ephrah,[1] all they from Sheba shall come; they shall bring gold and incense and they shall show forth the praises of the Lord. (See figure 11.)

In the Qu'ran, when King Solomon questioned the hoopoe bird about where he had been, the bird said: "I have seen a land ruled by a Queen who worships the sun. She possesses a magnificent throne, and is pro-

---

[1]Ephrah is a son of Midian according to Genesis 25:4.

vided with every requisite" (S XVII 23–24). In the land of Sheba, gold and silver are as dung in the street, says the hud-hud bird in Targum Sheni, a later Jewish Midrash of the Bible story. The hoopoe bird's description of Sheba was later confirmed by the archaeologists. Buildings were faced with gold and silver. There was, indeed, plenty of it.

In the first century A.D., Pliny the Elder and Diodorus Siculus as well, described Sheba's way of life:

They have embossed goblets of every description, made of silver and gold, couches and tripods with silver feet, and every other furnishing of incredible costliness, and halls circled by large columns, some of them gilded, and others having silver figures on their capitals. Their ceilings and doors they partitioned by means of panels and coffers made of gold, set with precious stones and placed close together, and have thus made the structure of their houses in every part marvelous for its costliness; for some parts they have constructed of silver and gold, others of ivory and the most showy precious stones or of whatever else men esteem most highly (S III 47:5–8).

A major factor in the development of the land of Sheba was its self-sufficiency in agriculture and commerce, combined with its total isolation fourteen hundred miles south of Palestine and the great empires to the north. The land between is rugged, barren, almost waterless desert. The coast of the Gulf of Aden to the south, and both sides of the Red Sea bordering Sheba on the west, are treacherous with coral reefs, and in ancient times, pirates. This isolation enabled the Sabeans to live in safety and security, free of the military devastations exchanged regularly between the northern countries. Any foreign influences that were brought into Sheba came through Sabean-dominated trade and were selected by the Sabeans themselves, not imposed upon them by conquerors. Thus, the culture and civilization of Sheba was purely Sheba's. While Solomon's reign was a time of peace in an otherwise turbulent place, Sheba's land was timeless in its peacefulness.

Not surprisingly, Sheba was ruled by Queens much more frequently than by Kings. Since there was no need for a military leader, matriarchal succession was preferred. Motherhood is certain—fatherhood is not. During the reign of the Queen of Sheba in the tenth century B.C., her land enjoyed an unparalleled time of prosperity. Perhaps because the Queen of Sheba and her people worshipped the Sun, the Moon, the stars and the planets, they were able to use their appreciation of these natural elements in their own kingdom and in their commercial travels. The Queen of Sheba was a *Mukarrib*, or high priestess. The word means "bringer of unity," and kindred of the Moon. The Hebrew word *kerubh*, cherub, and *kerubim*, cherubim, has the same root meaning. The Arabic word *muquaribim*, meaning close kindred, was the name for medieval Sufi mystics. So Sheba, as *Mukarrib*, understood the practical marriage of water and earth very well, and knew the magic of fire and air and their uses with incense, and how to use the gum resins of trees as antidotes to poison, for healing and beauty, for the preservation of bodies for

Figure 12. The Timna lions and a male rider. This is a superb example of ancient bronze sculpture that probably symbolizes the subjugation of the Sun God to the Moon God.

the afterlife, and above all as a sacrifice to the Gods, a way of making one's prayers ascend to God, Allah.

The arts, architecture, and calligraphy of Sheba were highly developed and characterized by balance, symmetry, proportion and grace. People dressed in linen garments, and women used bronze mirrors and alabaster cosmetic boxes and palettes in their beauty rituals. Men wore thin and gracefully stylized beards with and without moustaches. The language spoken during the reign of the Queen of Sheba is a dialect of South Arabia of which the major modern survivor is Ethiopic. It was written by the highly literate people of Sheba in an elegant monumental style, using somewhat elongated letters formed with clean and simple lines.

The land of Sheba abounded in sculpture, both in stone and bronze. It was more abundant in these arts than any other country in the ancient Near East. Virtually all sculpture was made for religious purposes. Sensitively rendered, realistically proportioned, detailed bulls were carved with crescent shaped horns symbolizing the Moon God. Ibexes and rams were sculpted with graceful arching horns much larger and more curving than they are in reality to honor the Moon. Friezes of rows of ibexes were often surmounted with the motif of cherubim with human heads, bodies of lions and wings of large birds. The cherubim stood with one foot planted on the fronds of a palm tree and the other on the ground.

The Sun God Shams, or Sin, was represented by squarish lions, sculpted in the round. Pritchard describes a spectacular bronze composed of two lions each with a male baby rider (see figure 12) in his *Solomon and Sheba*. The babies hold the subjugated lions by

Figure 13. A gold necklace from the Timna Cemetery. The name Hagarlat 'Alay Far'at is probably that of the woman to whom it belonged. The Moon Mother Bilqis is one of Sheba's names.

means of a chain in one hand which is attached to the animal's collar, and carry a stick or a dart in the other hand. He suggests that the motif symbolizes the supremacy of the Moon God, represented by the male babies, over the Sun God, represented by the lions. Though this particular bronze was made after the reign

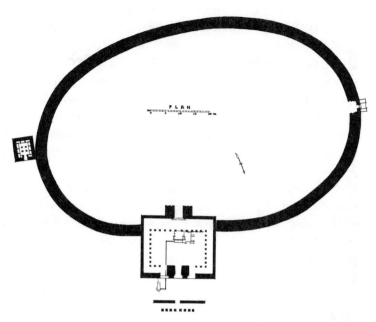

Figure 14. The Temple of Ilmugah, the Moon God, at Marib. This temple was popularly known as the Temple of Bilqis.

of the Queen of Sheba, Pritchard claims that it does represent the content of religious thought in Sheba.[2]

The motif of the crescent Moon itself was used in jewelry and amulets then as it is now (see figure 13).

The oldest temple in the land of Sheba is called Mahram Bilqis, meaning Moon Mother Bilqis, the pre-

---

[2]See *Solomon and Sheba*, edited by James B. Pritchard (London: Phaidon Press, 1974), p. 56.

cincts of the Queen of Sheba at Marib (see figure 14, page 33). It is an oval building with only one entrance. In this doorway is a large bronze basin filled with water, which one had to walk through in order to enter the central oval chamber. The cistern was fed by an underground well and the overflow of water was carried away by a channel that crossed the main chamber. Once again, one sees the close correspondence between ablution with water and religious worship of the Moon God as it occurred in Sheba's land.

Psychologically, one could say the land of Sheba was isolated, introverted, self-sufficient, and perhaps overly contained. Folklore pictures the Queen of Sheba before her visit to Jerusalem as a pathologically shy virgin, unawakened, and identified with being in and of her own land.

We have, then, a rich and powerful King in Jerusalem and an equally wealthy and secure Queen in Sheba. What in the world or the unseen would ever have caused these two to meet?

Chapter 3

THE NEED –
THE CALL

The Old Testament, patriocentric as it is, says that the Queen of Sheba, having heard of Solomon's wealth and wisdom, came to test him with hard questions (Kings 10:1–14). The Qur'an tells it another way. Solomon, having heard of the land of Sheba ruled by a woman, where gold and silver were as plentiful as dust, and where people worshipped the Sun and the Moon, summoned the Queen to Jerusalem (S XXVII 23–24). A third version, the Kebra Nagast, the holy book of the Ethiopians, is perhaps best because it seems the only one of the three to truly explain why these two ruling principles – monarchs – each ensconced in his and her own land far from each other geographically, and so completely opposite in so many other respects, *had* to meet – it was God's will.

According to the Kebra Nagast (xlviii), God wished to transfer the kingdom of David from Jerusalem to Ethiopia. In order to accomplish this, Sheba and Solomon had to meet, and eventually, have a son. He was called Ben 'l Halim in Hebrew, or Ibn l'Hakim in Arabic, and Menyelek in Ethiopian, Son of the Wise Man. It was Menyelek who stole the Tabernacle of Zion from Jerusalem and carried it off to Ethiopia. The object was to keep the God of Israel in Ethiopia. The original Zion existed in an immaterial form in heaven. In it dwelt God and His feminine side, the Shekhina. Moses made a copy of it in gold and wood (xlii) under divine direction and placed in it the Tablets of Law, the Ten Commandments, the pot of manna, and Aaron's rod.

This material copy was called "Zion, the Tabernacle of the Law of God." When Solomon finished building the Temple, Zion was established there in the Holy of Holies, and from it God made known His commands when He visited the temple. It was at all times held to be the visible emblem and the material duplicate of the immaterial Zion in heaven of God Almighty. Menyelek did, indeed, bring the Tabernacle of Zion to Ethiopia and established the rule there of Solomonic kings who were also Gods, since Christ was descended from Solomon, and he was the Son of God. Thus the king of Ethiopia, being a kinsman of Christ, was also a son of God and therefore both a God and a king to his people.

Even with the underlying understanding that it was God's will that Solomon and Sheba should meet, one might still ask "why" the Queen of Sheba left her land of plenty, so seemingly self-sufficient, self-sustaining and self-contained, and undertook a long and arduous journey to visit with the wise King Solomon. The Old Testament is most obvious and concise in its familiar explanation. Hearing of Solomon's wealth and wisdom, she came to test him with hard questions and to see with her own eyes whether what she had heard was true. From this point of view there seems to be a state of lack on Sheba's part. Even if it was merely curiosity that motivated her, it was an opening, a sign of need. There was something missing in her own land. She had to go there to Solomon's realm to find out what she needed to

Figure 15. The Queen of Sheba offers gifts to Solomon. Created prior to 1588, Pinacoteca, Turin, by Paolo Veronese. (From *Solomon and Sheba*, edited by J. B. Pritchard, Phaidon Press, London, 1974.)

know. Sheba's words to Solomon, "I did not believe until I saw with my own eyes . . ." suggests that much more than curiosity was at stake. There was a need to *experience* the truth, to confirm reality with her own being instead of relying upon hearsay and imagination. The meeting itself—of Sheba coming to Solomon—is a frequent subject for Christian painters (see figure 15 on page 37).

The Kebra Nagast tells the story of how the Queen of Sheba had heard of Solomon from one of her subjects, a merchant named Tamrin:

Now at that time King SOLOMON wished to build the House of God, and he sent out messages among all the merchants in the east and in the west, and in the north and in the south, bidding the merchants come and take gold and silver from him, so that he might take from them whatsoever was necessary for the work. And certain men reported to him concerning this rich ETHIOPIAN merchant, and SOLO-MON sent to him a message and told him to bring whatsoever he wished from the country of ARABIA, red gold, and black wood that could not be eaten by worms, and sapphires. And that merchant, whose name was TAMRIN, a merchant of the Queen of SHEBA, went to SOLOMON the King; and SOLOMON took whatsoever he desired from him, and he gave to the merchant whatsoever he wished for in great abundance. Now that merchant was a man of great understanding, and he saw and comprehended the wisdom of SOLOMON, and he marvelled thereat, and he watched carefully so that he might learn how the King made answer by his word, and understand his judgement, and the readiness of his mouth, and the discreetness of his speech, and the manner of his life, and his sitting down and his rising up, and his occupations, and his love, and his administration, and his table, and his law. To those to whom SOLOMON had to give orders he spake with humility and graciousness, and when they had committed a fault he admonished them gently. For he ordered his house in the wisdom and fear of God, and he smiled graciously on the fools and set them on the right road, and he dealt gently with the maidservants. He opened his mouth in parables, and his words were sweeter than the purest honey; his whole behavior was admirable, and his whole aspect pleasant. For wisdom is beloved by men of understanding, and is rejected by fools.

And when that merchant had seen all these things he was astonished, and he marvelled exceedingly (Kebra Nagast 22).

When Tamrin returned to his own country he told the Queen all that he had seen of the wisdom of Solomon:

. . . how he administered judgement and did what was just, and how he ordered his table, and how he made feasts, and how he taught wisdom, and how he directed his servants and all his affairs on a wise system, and how they went on their errands at his command, and how no man defrauded another, and how no man purloined the property of his neighbour, and how there was neither a thief nor a robber in his days. For in his wisdom he knew those who had done wrong, and he chastised them, and made them afraid, and they did not repeat their evil deeds, but they lived in a state of peace which had mingled therein the fear of the King.

All these things did TAMRIN relate unto the Queen, and each morning he recalled the things that he had seen with the King and described them unto her. And the Queen was struck dumb with wonder at the things that she heard from the merchant her servant, and she thought in her heart that she would go to him; and she wept by reason of the greatness of her pleasure in those things that TAMRIN had told her (Kebra Nagast 23).

So Sheba received her information about Solomon's world from this merchant who had traveled abroad, and thought in her heart that she would go and see for herself.

And she was exceedingly anxious to go to him, but when she pondered upon the long journey she thought that it was too far and too difficult to undertake. And time after time she asked

TAMRIN questions about SOLOMON, and time after time TAMRIN told her about him, and she became very wishful and most desirous to go that she might hear his wisdom, and see his face, and embrace him, and petition his royalty. And her heart inclined to go to him, for God had made her heart incline to go and had made her desire it (Kebra Nagast 23).

Here Sheba is very like modern women who have had careers in the world and been quite successful, but at some point realize, or are forced to realize, that they have been in the world using only their masculine side, while they, themselves, as women have remained "at home," unawakened, virginal, and inexperienced. These mid-career crises—while very painful, often frightening, difficult, confusing and worse—often result in real transformation, as this does for Sheba.

And the Queen said,"Hearken, O ye who are my people, and give ye ear to my words. For I desire wisdom and my heart seeketh to find understanding. I am smitten with the love of wisdom, and I am constrained by the cords of understanding; for wisdom is far better than treasure of gold and silver, and wisdom is the best of everything that hath been created on the earth. Now unto what under the heavens shall wisdom be compared? It is sweeter than honey, and it maketh one to rejoice more than wine, and it illumineth more than the sun, and it is to be loved more than precious stones. And it fatteneth more than oil, and it satisfieth more than dainty meats, and it giveth more renown than treasure of gold and silver. It is a source of joy for the heart, and a bright and shining light for the eyes, and a giver of speed to the feet, and a shield for the breast, and a helmet for the head, and chain-work for the neck, and a belt for the loins. Wisdom is an exalted thing and a rich thing: I will love her like a mother, and she shall embrace me like her child. I will follow the foot-prints of wisdom and she shall protect me for ever; I will seek after wisdom, and she shall be with me for ever; I will follow her footprints, and she shall not cast me away; I will lean upon her, and she shall be unto me a wall of adamant; I will seek asylum with her, and she shall be unto me power and strength; I will rejoice in her, and she shall be unto me abundant grace. For it is right for us to follow the footprints of wisdom, and for the soles of our feet to stand upon the threshold of the gates of wisdom. Let us seek her, and we shall find her; let us love her, and she will not withdraw herself from us; let us pursue her, and we shall overtake her; let us ask, and we shall receive; and let us turn our heart to her so that we may never forget her. If we remember her, she will have us in remem-brance and in connection with fools thou shalt not remember wisdom, for they do not hold her in honour, and she doth not love them.

Although Tamrin has described over and over again to the Queen of Sheba the wonders of Solomon's court and realm and law, administration, wealth, wisdom and power, Sheba's intuitive imagination leads her to say to her people this extraordinary thing: "I am smitten with the love of wisdom. It is a source of joy for the heart. *I will love her like a mother, and she shall embrace me like her child.*" Mother Wisdom will provide a path and a way and much, much more. Then, Sheba adds:

> The honouring of wisdom is the honouring of the wise man, and the loving of wisdom is the loving of the wise man. Love the wise man and withdraw not thyself from him, and by the sight of him thou shalt become wise; hearken to the utterance of his mouth, so that thou mayest become like unto him; watch the place whereon he hath set his foot, and leave him not, so that thou mayest receive the remainder of his wisdom. And I love him merely on hearing concerning him and without seeing him, and the whole story of him that hath been told me is to me as the desire of my heart, and like water to the thirsty man.

> And her nobles, and her slaves, and her handmaidens, and her counsellors answered and said unto her, "O our Lady, as for wisdom, it is not lacking in thee, and it is because of thy wisdom that thou lovest wisdom. And as for us, if thou goest we will go with thee, and if thou sittest down we will sit down with thee; our death shall be with thy death, and our life with thy life." Then the Queen made ready to set out on her journey with great pomp and majesty,

Figure 16. A modern Israeli artist's fantastic rendition of a goat-footed woman, who could easily be Sheba. (Drawing by David Tsur, from the author's collection.)

and with great equipment and many prepara-
tions. For, by the Will of God, her heart desired
to go to JERUSALEM so that she might hear the
wisdom of SOLOMON; for she had harkened
eagerly. So she made ready to set out. And
seven hundred and ninety-seven camels were
loaded, and mules and asses innumerable were
loaded, and she set out on her journey and followed her road without pause, and her heart
had confidence in God (Kebra Nagast 24).

So clearly, the Queen of Sheba was an explorer at heart.
She set out in answer to her heart's longing, and her
love of wisdom, and her need to taste it and experience
it directly.

The Kebra Nagast further elaborates on the sense of
a lack, or need, on the part of the Queen of Sheba:

And behold (xlviii Kebra Nagast), from the ear-
liest times the Land of Sheba was ruled over by
royal princesses. When the mother of this
Queen of Sheba was with child she saw a fat
and handsome looking goat, and she looked
upon him with greedy desire, and said, "How
handsome the beast is! And how handsome its
feet are!" She longed for it after the manner of
women who are with child. When the aforementioned daughter was fashioned completely
in the womb of her mother, she had one foot
like the foot of a human being, and another like
the foot of a goat. Great and exalted be the Creator of the Universe, Who is to be praised!
When the mother of the Queen had brought

forth this extraordinary being, and had reared
her until she was old enough to marry, the
maiden did not wish to marry any man because
of her malformed foot. She continued in her
virginity until she began to reign.

The thought to visit Solomon to hear his wisdom arose in her mind, as has already been
mentioned because it had been ordained in the
wisdom of God, praise be to Him. When the
aforementioned Queen arrived in Jerusalem,
and Solomon the king had heard of it, and was
quite certain from the information, which he
had received from spies, that one of her feet
was the foot of a goat, he planned a cunning
plan in his wisdom, whereby he might be able
to see her foot without having to ask her to
show it to him. He placed his throne by the side
of the courtyard of the Temple, and ordered his
servants to open the sluices so that the courtyard would be filled with water. This was done
and the aforementioned piece of wood, having
been brought there by the mother rukh bird
from below Paradise, was submerged by the
water, but no one noticed this thing which had
been decreed aforetime by the wisdom of God.
    When the Queen of Sheba arrived, she
drew up the lower parts of her cloak and garments beneath it so that she might step into the
water. Thus, Solomon saw her foot. And
behold, she stepped into the water in the courtyard, and her foot that was fashioned like the
foot of a goat touched the aforementioned piece

of wood, the Might of God made itself manifest and the malformed foot became exactly like her human foot.

One might surmise that the Queen of Sheba *needed* to go to Jerusalem in order to be healed of her malformed foot. Or more conservatively one could say that she had a problem, that of the foot, a feeling of woundedness, which kept her from an intimate relationship with a man and predisposed her to seek out Solomon's wisdom. (See figure 17, page 48.) Psychologically, one might say that this mother's lustfulness had been compensated by the daughter's shame. Sheba sought Solomon's wisdom for help in understanding this matter, or accepting it, and was forced to at least reveal the problem by his cunning wisdom.

The Qur'an may well be the source for this part of this story. In it, the Queen of Sheba mistakes the glass or crystal floor of Solomon's palace for a lake of water and lifts her skirts as she enters his throne room (fig. 18, page 50). Solomon, perhaps feeling this to be a very undignified position for a woman, especially a queen, immediately says: "This is but a palace paved smooth with slabs of glass" (S XXVII 44). Sheba's response is quite extraordinary. She said, "O my Lord! I have indeed wronged my soul: I do now submit in Islam with Solomon to the Lord of the Worlds." So while the ending of the story is the same in both instances, and one can sense the relief Sheba finds in Jerusalem, the Qur'an does not really elucidate her woundedness or need as a reason for her going there.

While the Bible and the Kebra Nagast emphasize Sheba's need to go to Jerusalem, the Qur'an elucidates

Figure 17. The Queen of Sheba exposes her legs to Solomon. (From Majalis Al-Ushshq, a 16th century collection of amulets from the British Library, Or MS 11837, Folio 162v.)

Solomon's need for meeting Sheba. The entire story of Solomon and Sheba is told in the Sura of the Ant (XXVII). There is, first of all, a lovely introduction, saying that:

> These are verses
> Of the Qur'an—a Book
> That makes things clear;
>
> A Guide and Glad Tidings
> For the Believers.

We know that although Solomon is a believer, and, in the Qur'an even a prophet of God, he had, on the human level, doubts and lapses. He married foreign women in order to obtain knowledge of their gods, and he worshipped idols in the high places. So this preamble to the story of his encounter with Sheba must be viewed in this light. It continues, saying that sometimes people are so pleased with their own deeds that they go about distracted from the Divine source of this creative ability. Psychologically, one sees a narcissistic overvaluing of one's own accomplishments, idol worshipping of the material world, a confusion of ego with Self, a use of power and control that is despotic and evil because it is godless. The Sura of the Ants continues, telling the story of how Moses, while traveling in the desert with his family seeking the ordinary light and warmth of a fire, was given an inner light (or consciousness) which showed him the highest mysteries of God. Then his ordinary rod or staff, a dead piece of wood that had hitherto supported him, was transformed into a serpent, instinct with life and movement, potent with the

Figure 18. Bilqis sees the fish below the glass pavement and instinctively raises her skirts to show her legs to Solomon. (From Bodleian Library, Oxford, MS Ouseley ADD 24 folio 1270.)

abilities of offense and defense. Moses was at first frightened by this divine intervention and new insight, as are most people when they first see something of this intensity and experience a deepening of their own instinctual life and consciousness of God's nature in all this. The third sign given Moses was that God instructed him that if anyone had done wrong by their own hand, substituting bad deeds for good, they should put their hand on their heart, and God could forgive them (S XVII 11–13). The Qur'an says (S XXVII 13–15):

> But when our Signs come
> to them, that should have
> Opened their eyes, they said:
> "This is sorcery manifest!"
> And they rejected these Signs
> In iniquity and arrogance,
> Though their souls were convinced
> Thereof: so see what was the
> end of those
> Who acted corruptly!

So the Qur'an sets the background for the story of Solomon and Sheba, and continues:

> We gave in the past
> Knowledge to David and Solomon;
> And they both said:
> "Praise be to God, Who
> Has favored us above many
> Of His servants who believe!

But the Bible, though it calls David "a man after God's own heart" (I Samuel 13:14, and Acts 13:22), also describes his crimes of adultery and murder, and speaks also of Solomon's lapses into idolatry and sin. The Qur'an continues (S XXVII 16–19):

> And Solomon was David's heir.
> He said: 'O ye people!
> We have been taught the speech
> Of Birds, and on us had been bestowed a little
> Of all things: this is
> Indeed Grace manifest from God.'
> And before Solomon were marshalled
> His hosts—of djinns and men
> And birds, and they were all
> Kept in order and in ranks.
>
> At length when they came
> To a lowly valley of ants,
> One of the ants said:
> O ye ants, get into your habitations,
>   lest Solomon
> And his hosts crush you
> Underfoot without knowing it.
>
> So he smiled, amused
> At her speech; and he said:
> "O my Lord! so order me
> That I may be grateful
> For thy favors. . . .

So here we have Solomon, knowledgable, powerful, and lordly, made grateful and aware of God's gifts by the tiny instinctual ant whose diligence, order, and communication skills are mirrors of his own abilities. The story continues: Solomon had gathered all his minions around him—the birds, the beasts, and the djinns—but he noticed that the hoopoe bird was missing. Symbolically this is, indeed, a severe lack. The hoopoe is a bird that is reputed to be able to find water, a most valuable substance in that part of the world. Moreover it has on its breast the Symbol of the Spirits' Way, and on its head Truth's crown, and most significant of all, on its beak a holy sign: the word *Bismillah* is forever etched, which means in Arabic, "In the name of God." Attar in his famous mystical poem, *The Conference of the Birds*,[1] tells of the hoopoe as the spiritual gatherer and guide of all the birds, or wayward egocentric elements in mankind, and how the hoopoe brings them all to the knowledge of God. In the Qur'an it is the hoopoe or Bismillah bird that brings Sheba to Solomon's attention, saying, "I have found a place that you, Solomon, however wise and wealthy, know nothing of (S XXVII 23):

I have come to thee
From Sheba with tidings true.
I found there a woman
Ruling over them and provided
With every requisite; and she
Has a magnificent throne.

By now the hoopoe has easily piqued Solomon's interest. The historical account of the Old Testament

---

[1]See Farid ud-Din Attar: *Conference of the Birds* (New York: Viking Penguin, 1984), Tr. by Afkham Darbandi and Dick Davis.

has shown that Solomon was placed on his throne by the intervention of his mother, Bathsheba. And she had become his father's lover while she was still married to Uriah the Hittite. David had been attracted to her when he saw her bathing and called her to his bed. After she became pregnant with his child he had had her husband, a loyal military leader for David, killed. For this sin David and Bathsheba suffered the death of their first child. Solomon was the only surviving fruit of their union. He wrote of himself in his Song of Songs, 3:11:

> Daughters of Zion,
> come and see
> King Solomon,
> wearing the diadem with which
> his mother crowned him. . . .

So we see that Solomon felt himself to have been empowered by his mother, further explaining his dream at Gibeon where he expresses his feeling that compared to his father King David, he feels as a little child who "knows not when to come in and when to go out."

Moreover the Queen of Sheba, who rules in her own right, has every requisite as Solomon has, including a magnificent throne, which as we shall see becomes an object of great fascination to Solomon.

The hoopoe continues to excite Solomon's interest (S XXVII 24):

> I found her and her people
> Worshipping the sun besides God.

In fact, the people of Sheba worshipped Sun, Moon, planets and stars, and Solomon's wish to learn of these religions through sexual congress with the women who practiced them has been well documented. The hoopoe continues:

> Satan has made their deeds
> Seem pleasing in their eyes,
> And has kept them away
> From the Path, — so
> They receive no guidance, —

The bird makes Solomon aware that the Sabeans have mistaken their superb material achievements to be theirs alone on an ego level, and that they have lost sight of the one true "God who brings to light what is hidden in the heavens and the earth, and knows what ye hide and what ye reveal." The bird avers:

> God! — there is no god
> But He! — Lord of the Throne
> Supreme! (S XXVII 25–27)

Solomon's interest is piqued. He immediately writes a letter summoning the Queen of Sheba to Jerusalem and says to the hoopoe (S XXVII 28):

> Go thou, with this letter
> Of mine, and deliver it
> To them: then draw back
> From them, and wait to see
> What answer they return.

And so begin the games, a battle of wits between the King and the Queen (see figure 19, p. 57). There is an atmosphere of testing, a competition, curiosity and challenge on both sides.

One legend says that when the hoopoe arrived, knowing that the Queen prayed to the rising Sun at dawn, he blocked out her window with his wings, so that when Sheba rose for prayer she was terrified because there was no Sun. Another story says that the hoopoe summoned legions of blackbirds to carpet the heavens so that Sheba could not see the Sun at all, and was frightened.

The Qur'an continues, saying that when the hoopoe arrived, the Queen read the letter to her chief advisors, asking for their advice, almost beseechingly, and somewhat alarmed by Solomon's aggressiveness (S XXVII 29–32).

> She said: "Ye chiefs!
> Here is — delivered to me —
> A letter worthy of respect.
> It is from Solomon and says
> (as follows): 'In the name
> Of God, Most Gracious, Most Merciful:
>
> Be ye not arrogant
> Against me, but come
> To me in submission . . .' "

The Queen of Sheba, perhaps frightened by this summons from Solomon speaking in God's name (figure 20, page 58), begs her advisors for help (S XXVII 32–33):

Figure 19. A) Solomon with his djinns—his birds—and his attendants (from British Library, Add MS 18579 Folio 368v); B) Solomon and the hoopoe bird. A page from Luqman-i Ashuri: *Subdat al Tawarikh* (a manuscript in the Chester Beatty Library, Dublin).

Figure 20. Bilqis, the Queen of Sheba, shown with the hoopoe bird perched on a tree with Solomon's letter in its beak (from the British Museum).

> She said: "Ye chiefs!
> Advise me in this
> My affair: no affair
> Have I decided
> Except in your presence."

Here again are echoes of the Kebra Nagast's report of the Queen's wounded foot, her feeling of inadequacy in dealing with men who are strangers, and her need to depend on her male advisors for help in this matter. Her own feminine standpoint—her foot—is crippled. She cannot stand on her own when faced by Solomon's aggressive summons to leave her own land; she is frightened. Indeed, she seems to be saying that even in domestic matters, never has she stood on her own and decided on her own. But the Qur'an shows how this healing of the feminine principle is begun by the coming of the call from God or the Self, via Solomon. The advisors say (S XXVII 33):

> We are endued
> With strength, and given
> To vehement war:
> But the command is
> With thee; so consider
> What thou wilt command.

The Queen of Sheba, perhaps empowered by this expression of confidence in her military power by her council of advisors, and even more so by their willing loyalty and reliance upon *her* judgment and command, takes heart. She begins to devise her own plan, using reason and feeling so that her power is both more sure-footed, from the goat foot side, and more balanced and secure in its effect, because she stands on two feet.

> She said: "Kings when they
> Enter a country, despoil it,
> And make the noblest
> Of its people its meanest;
> Thus do they behave.
>
> But I am going to send
> Him a present, and wait
> To see with what answer
> Return my ambassadors."
> (S XXVII 34)

So Sheba, with a certain womanly grace, steps aside from the demanding aggressive tone of Solomon's communique, thinking, war is hell, everyone loses, and decides to send him a present. She chooses to make love, not war. She is like Psyche in the Greek myth, who is helped in her task of gathering the Golden Fleece from the rams by the whispering reeds who tell her that the rams are maddened by the heat of the sun and rage about all day batting heads and fighting with each other. When the sun goes down—in the cool of the lunar light—they rest and then one can easily gather the fleece from the twigs and branches where it is caught.

But Solomon is not so easily mollified; in fact he takes her gift to him in the worst possible way. He said (S XXVII 36):

> Will ye give me abundance
> In wealth? But that which
> God has given me is better
> Than that which He has
> Given you! Nay it is ye
> Who rejoice in your gift!

So he thinks she is showing off, and defensively, rather obviously betraying his own feelings of inadequacy, says (S XXVII 37):

> Go back to them, and be sure
> We shall come to them
> With such hosts as they
> Will never be able to meet:
> We shall expel them
> From there in disgrace,

And they will feel
Humbled indeed.

Seemingly quieted by this outburst, Solomon seems to
drop the outwardly warlike approach and says to his
own men:

Ye chiefs! which of you
Can bring me her throne
Before they come to me
In submission?
Said an Ifrit, of the djinns:
"I will bring it to thee
Before thou rise from thy
Council: indeed I have

Full strength for the purpose,
And may be trusted."
(S XXVII 38–40)

An Ifrit is a large and powerful djinn reputed to be
wicked and crafty, hence he is anxious to be trusted. But
(S XXVII 40):

Said one who had knowledge
Of the Book: "I will
Bring it to thee within
The twinkling of an eye!"
Then when Solomon saw it
Placed firmly before him,
He said: "This is
By the grace of my Lord! —
To test whether I am
Grateful or ungrateful!"

The big Ifrit had boasted of his brute strength, as had Solomon in his aggressive posturing, but this is not enough to transform a power throne based on materialism into one based on inward knowledge. This inner understanding and true power is a throne of the heart and spirit and comes from knowledge of the Book of the Grace of God. The magic of spiritual love acts in the twinkling of an eye. Solomon has remembered his father in God and chooses his course, but the stage is now set for the meeting and mutual testing of each of these two ruling principles. Clearly, each has felt the call of the Self, and the need for this encounter to deal with a spiritual problem. Where does one's ego accomplishments fall short? Where—despite material wealth and power—does one feel empty, something missing? Whether overreaching and overly identified with doing—like Solomon, or constricted and contained and overly identified with being—like Sheba, ego longs for Self. Each monarch is wounded, curious, competitive, frightened, needy, accomplished, able, and distrustful.

Chapter 4

THE TESTING
OF HEARTS

Thus far we have seen that though both Solomon and Sheba are effective popular rulers on the external plane, each suffers from certain inner conflicts and even spiritual malaise in regard to the opposite sex. Solomon marries foreign women to gain access to their gods, and Sheba is afraid to marry at all, so estranged is she from her masculine side. Each has projected the divine elements of the contrasexual side onto the other. Each believes the other has the secret knowledge, real power and the true throne. Culturally, psychologically, one sees this all the time; accomplished, successful women who feel unfulfilled, inadequate, ashamed and unloved if they are unmarried. And accomplished, successful men who cannot love, and feel unfulfilled, depressed and angry, married or not. Central to this problem is the question of the heart's desire. "A crucible for silver, a furnace for gold, but Yahweh for the testing of hearts!" (Proverbs of Solomon 17:3).

At conception, perhaps, each person is most whole, complete, contained and full of potential; some people believe, even closest to God. Qabalists say that on the night before birth the little soul is carried all over heaven and earth by an angel of God. It learns all there is to know. The light of knowing burns brightly in its face. Just before it is put back into its mother's womb, the light is extinguished, thus the tiny depression at the base of the infant's nose and peak of its lips. From birth on, one searches for this feeling of knowing God, of completion and divine love. Often, doing is thought to

Figure 21. The Queen of Sheba comes to prove Solomon with hard questions. (Mansell Collection)

be a way to attain or restore the lost sense of fulfillment. Getting and having, the other two idols of the material world, are worshipped also, but at a certain point, often not till midlife, a person realizes that something is very wrong. Something is missing—for Solomon it was the hoopoe who had found a secret feminine realm, unknown to Solomon. For Sheba it was hearing of the wise and wealthy masculine principle and feeling threatened by it. Each had always distrusted the other sex. (See figure 21 on page 64.) One may view Solomon developmentally, both by his own writings, and the historical accounts given in the Old Testament books of II Samuel and I Kings. In Wisdom 7:1–6 Solomon writes:

> Like all the others I too am a mortal man, descendant of the first fashioned from the earth, I was modelled in flesh in my mother's womb, for ten lunar months taking shape in her blood by means of virile seed and pleasure, sleep's companion. I too, when I was born, drew in the common air, I fell on the same ground that bears us all, a wail my first sound, as for all the rest. I was nurtured in swaddling clothes, with every care. No king has known any other beginning of existence; for all there is one way only into life, as out of it.

Solomon, as we know, was the second son of an adulterous pair. He was conceived in a womb recently vacated by a baby who died for his parents' sins. His mother, Bathsheba, was not the first nor the last wife of his father, David, and he grew up in court full of intrigue, incest, and innuendo. Solomon's contempt for the feminine is demonstrated by the legend that when he was 3, his mother threatened to have him killed for saying that a woman's soul has no more significance than a curl of wood shaving. Bathsheba's overreaction is suggestive of her heartless mothering. When Solomon was a boy, Amnon, one of his half brothers, raped Tamar, one of his half sisters. Tamar's twin brother Absalom was David's favorite son. Absalom killed the rapist, breaking his father's heart, and ran away. Eventually, Absalom died hanging by his hair from a branch of a tree where he was caught while fleeing. It was into this void in the succession to David's kingship that Bathsheba pushed Solomon. The attitude toward women illustrated in this story of Solomon at 3, continues in his Book of Proverbs where he relegates women to being either a crown to their husbands or dangerous seductresses: "A gracious woman brings honor to her husband, she who has no love for justice is dishonor enthroned" (11:16). And, "A golden ring in the snout of a pig is a lovely woman who lacks discretion" (11:22). Similarly, "A good wife her husband's crown, a shameless wife, a cancer in his bones. A perfect wife—who can find her? She is far beyond the price of pearls" (31:10). In Ecclesiasticus (7:26–29), Solomon writes: "I find woman more bitter than death; she is a snare, her heart a net, her arms are chains; He who is pleasing to God eludes her, but the sinner is her captive. This then you must know, is the sum of my investigations, putting this and that together. I have made other researches too, without result. One man in a thousand I may find, but never a woman better than the rest." "Do not give your soul to a woman, for her to trample on your strength" (9:2)—and he follows this advice with warnings against "harlots, singing girls, virgins, whores, letting one's eyes wander in infrequented quarters, handsome women, beautiful women, married women and charming women" (9:3–10)!

This is the man who summons the virgin Queen of Sheba. Her history is more of a mystery. In the Book of Genesis (25:6), Abraham's sons by Keturah from which descend the Arabian tribes, include Jokshan, father of Sheba (Genesis 25:3).

The oral tradition of both the Jewish and Arabic world and the Stories of the Prophet hold that the mother of the Queen of Sheba was a demon. Her father was a vassal of the King of Sheba who played the game of propounding riddles to great men of his court and, after a fixed period, seizing their wealth when they were unable to answer. The Queen of Sheba's father had failed to answer a riddle and was given a test which if performed would bring clemency, and if not, death. In the course of this trial—to make a journey of three months in thirty days—the courtier had spied two serpents, one black and one white, in mortal combat. He killed the black serpent with a diamond pointed arrow and saved the life of the white serpent and completed his journey.

On his return trip he was greeted by a princely figure, who revealed that he was the white serpent and a djinn who was now desirous of repaying the courtier for his help by giving him the hand of the djinn's sister in marriage. He was captivated by her beauty and in marrying her had to agree not to question any of her acts. On their return to Sheba he was received with honor and with the help of his djinni wife who was as wise as she was beautiful, he answered all the king's riddles and saved the lives of all his fellow courtiers. His wife gave birth to a daughter even more beautiful and wise than her mother, and when she was 12, the King asked for her hand in marriage, made her his consort, placed a crown upon her head and declared her sovereign while he yet lived. When her mother died she became sovereign of the djinn as well, and following the death of the king, reigned in his place.

Another slightly different Turkish source says that Sheba's mother, the djinni, bore her husband, the King of Sheba, a son first, but when a dog approached her she threw the baby to him and allowed it to run off with it. Then she gave birth to a girl child but flung her into a blazing fire. A second daughter was as beautiful as the houris of Paradise. The king asked his wife not to treat her like the others, and for this she rebuked him, but she did destroy his enemies. When he again questioned her, she ended their marriage, but the king looked after their beautiful daughter until his death.

There is another much more alarming version of the story of how the Queen came to rule the people of Sheba. Her father, it is said, had been king and she was his only child, but when he died only some of the people supported her, while many others supported a male claimant to the throne. This claimant gained power, but acted harshly and pursued the wives of his subjects. They by then would have liked to dispose of him but were afraid to do so. To everyone's surprise, the princess hinted that she would like to marry him and he proposed. On their wedding night she made him drunk and cut off his head. On the following day all the people of Sheba acknowledged her as their Queen.

Most of these stories consider the Queen of Sheba's mother to be demonic, and her father to be quite heroic, thus fitting consistently with the Kebra Nagast tale of the Queen's mother, while pregnant, coveting a goat, thereby causing her daughter to be born with a deformed goat foot. The projection of a demonic feminine genealogy onto the Queen of Sheba is frequent in both Jewish and Islamic folklore. She is seen as having both hairy legs and feet, and sometimes a deformed animal foot. The animal foot and her matrilineal descent lead, also, to her identification with Lilith, an animal-footed demon, a seductive, child killing night-stalker. Further confusion of these dark elements arises from the conflation of two motifs brought about by the similarity of the words *sa'ir* — meaning hairy, and *sa'r* — a goat demon. The "hairy one" (*sa'ir*) is the name given by the Hebrews to certain demons who, in particular, inhabit the desert.

So the Queen of Sheba, if she had heard of any of these projections upon her, or if indeed she had been born with a deformed foot would surely have been as deferential to her advisors and as eager to meet Solomon as the Qur'an describes her. In her background, too, like Solomon's, there seems to be a cold and power-seeking mother, dead siblings sacrificed by the parents' demonic behavior, and a relatively kingly father. It is the cold power-seeking of the mothers that makes for the secret distrust and insecurity of both Solomon and Sheba. Each feels unlovable because they were not loved by their mothers for themselves, but only as pawns in the mother's power-seeking. Sheba's wound may be even deeper because her mother didn't seem to need her in this regard either, and perhaps abandoned her entirely, when she was questioned by her husband, and she returned to her demonic origins.

The Qur'an contains the story of Solomon's summons to Sheba and his testing of her, but this version seems to be based on earlier Jewish sources such as the Alphabet Ben Sira, the *Targum Sheni* and Josephus' *Antiquities of the Jews* 8:165–73. Here the story parallels the tale in the Book of Esther and begins with King Solomon's insecurity and his need to demonstrate his power and authority.

> Solomon, his heart made merry with wine, commands that harps, cymbals, drums, and lyres upon which his father, David, used to play, should be brought to him. While he was still of good cheer by reason of wine, Solomon summoned the beasts of the field, the birds of the air, the creeping reptiles, the shades, the spectres, the ghosts to dance and leap and bound, before the kings who were his friends and neighbors. Solomon wished to show the kings who were seated with him all his glory and his greatness. Solomon's scribes called the animals and spirits by name, one by one, and they all assembled of their own accord, without fetters or bonds, with no human bond to guide them.

Again one sees that while Solomon, gifted by God with wisdom, has regained the dominion over animals once held, then lost, by Adam by virtue of naming

them, Solomon, nevertheless, betrays his insecurity
among the other men—his peers. The Targum Sheni
continues:

> On one occasion the hoopoe or hud-hud bird
> was missing from among the birds. He could
> not be found anywhere. The king, full of wrath,
> ordered that he be brought before him and
> chastised. The hoopoe appeared and said:
>
> "O Lord, king of the world, incline thy ear and
> hearken to my words. Three months ago I
> began to take counsel with myself and admon-
> ish myself verily. I ate no food and drank no
> water. I resolved upon a course of action: to fly
> about in the whole world and see whether there
> is a domain anywhere which is not subject to
> my lord the king."

So again, as in the Qur'an, the Bismillah bird, the
testing, truth seeking, spiritual element, raises questions for Solomon. The hoopoe continues:

> I found in the East a city called Kitor, which
> means incense. Its earth is more valuable than
> gold, and silver is like odure in the streets. Its
> trees are from the beginning of all time. They
> were planted there in the six days of Creation
> and they drink the waters that flow from the
> Garden of Eden.

Jewish legend, as well as the Qur'an, links Sheba's land with the fecund creativity of Genesis. The bird continues rousing Solomon's curiosity and competition:

> The land is crowded with men. There is a great host and army and they wear golden crowns. Around their heads are garlands wreathed in Paradise. They know not how to wage war or smite nor how to shoot with bow and arrow, and there is no falsehood in their land.

This last, that there is no falseness, may have been the most potent hook to catch Solomon's interest thus far, but then the hoopoe says,

> Their ruler is a woman. She is called the Queen of Sheba. If, now, it please thee, O lord and king, I shall gird my loins like a warrior hero and fly to the city of Kitor in the land of Sheba. There I shall bind their kings in fetters and their honored ones in chains of iron and fetch them to my lord the king.

Solomon endorsed the plan and had a letter written and bound to the hoopoe's wing. He rose skyward, uttered his cry, mounted to the lofty heavens and flew off among all the other birds who followed him to the land of Sheba.

They arrived in early morning when the Queen had gone forth to prostrate herself and pay homage to the Sun, which was her custom. Suddenly the birds darkened the Sun's light. The Queen raised her hand and rent her garment and was sorely astonished. As she stood, frightened and astounded, *both* legs perhaps weakened and threatening to give way, the hoopoe delivered Solomon's letter:

> From me, King Solomon! Peace be with thee, peace with the nobles of thy realm! Know you not and have you not heard that the Holy and Blessed One has appointed me king over the beasts of the field, the birds of the air, the demons, the spirits and the spectres. All the kings of the East and the West, the North and the South come to bring me greetings. If you will come and salute me I will show you great honor, more than to any of the other kings who attend me. But if you will not pay homage to me, I will send out kings, legions and riders against you. If you ask who are these kings, legions and riders of King Solomon, then know you that the beasts of the field are my kings, the birds my riders, the demons, spirits and shades of the night my legions. The demons will throttle you in your bed at night, while the beasts will slay you in the field and the birds will consume your flesh.

The aggressiveness of Solomon's threat against a people who he has been told do not know how to wage war belies his fear of this strange land, ruled by a Queen. When the Queen of Sheba read the words of this epistle she took hold of her garments and rent them afresh.

In her fright she called for help from her advisors, but they knew nothing of Solomon and his realm and could not help her. So all on her own, she formulated her reply and began her form of testing: she assembled all the ships of the sea and had them loaded with the finest cypress wood and every kind of precious jewel, including according to some an unpierced pearl—with the *double entendre* such a gift implies. Together with these she sent Solomon six thousand youths and maidens, born in the same year, in the same month, on the same day, in the same hour, indeed at the same moment. They were all of equal height and stature, and all of them clad in purple.

There is a riddle inherent in this gift: how could all these children have been born in the same moment? The answer in light of feminine psychology seems obvious. Women living together in harmony tend to have the same menstrual cycles. The women of the land of Sheba, ruled by a queen, worshipping the moon at the temples of Marib and Timna and in harmony with nature, understood completely the connection between ovulation and conception. They ovulated at the same time and in good relation to their feminine natures made love when summoned by the heightened desirousness of ovulation and, thus, conceived and gave birth at the same time.

Neither the Qur'an nor the Old Testament tells of Solomon's ability to solve this riddle, nor do the collections of folklore that list the various riddles Solomon and Sheba are said to have asked of each other.

The queen put in the hands of these children her living riddle, a letter of her own, and sent it to King Solomon. It said, "From the land of Sheba to the land of Israel is a journey of seven years. As it is your wish and behest that I visit you, and since it is now my wish to see you face to face, I shall appear before you in three years time."

So the testing is in earnest now. The queen is engaged and demonstrates her own powers, as well. Some of the stories say she appeared in the twinkling of an eye, but these are the ones designed to demonstrate her demonic nature. A more practical explanation is that the Queen of Sheba had extensive trade routes in order to sell incense, and good working relations with the lands and people on her way, so she was able to travel quickly between stops. She obtained fresh camels and supplies at each staging area and thus completed her journey in a very short time. A more subtle explanation, offered by a perfumer and maker of attar and incense, is that whenever you burn incense, angels appear. The Queen of Sheba had much incense and many angels to carry her aloft, and they could carry her to Jerusalem in record time.

As she drew near to Jerusalem, Solomon again challenged her with a test of his own. He sent Benaiah Ben-Jehoiada to meet her:

> Benaiah was like the light that comes at the end of the morning watch, the flush in the Eastern sky at break of day, like the evening star that outshines all other stars, like the lily growing by brooks of water, and like the Hind of Dawn.

> When the Queen of Sheba, who was accustomed to worshipping the Sun, saw him, she descended from her chariot. Benaiah Ben-Jehoiada descended and said to her, "Why did you come down from your chariot?" And the

Queen answered, "Are you not King Solomon?" Benaiah answered, "I am not King Solomon but one of his servants who is seated
before him." Then the Queen turned to her
nobles and said, "If you have not beheld the
lion, at least you have seen his lair, and if you
have not seen King Solomon, at least you have
seen the beauty of him that stands in his
presence."

To pick up the tale as it proceeds in the Qur'an, Solomon has replied to the Queen's gifts saying (S XXVII
36):

Will ye give me abundance
In wealth? But that which
God has given me is better
Than that which He has
Given you! Nay it is ye
Who rejoice in your gifts!

Solomon's angry response may be defensive, but it
is also an accurate reading of the queen's intention to
show her own wealth and power. It is at this point that
Solomon asks to have the Queen's throne brought to
him (S XXVII 41).

He said: "Transform her throne
Out of all recognition by her:
Let us see whether she
Is guided (to the truth)
Or is one of those who
Receive no guidance."

King Solomon's throne is described in the Old Testament immediately following the description of the Queen of Sheba's visit and her gifts of gold, precious stones, incense and spices. Solomon, it says, received 666 talents of gold in one year. The three sixes are said to be an encoded allusion to the triple Goddess—the maid, mother, and crone—often represented as a triangle. From this gold Solomon made three hundred shields, each of three pounds of gold. And the Old Testament continues (I Kings 10:18),

> Moreover the king made a great throne of ivory and overlaid it with the finest gold. There were six steps to the throne, and the top of the throne was round behind; and there were arms on either side of the place of the seat, and two lions standing beside the arms. And twelve lions stood there on the one side and on the other upon the six steps; there was not the like made in any kingdom.

While the repeated use of threes may indeed refer to the Goddess, the gold and the lions are strongly solar and masculine in spirit (see figure 22, p. 78). Solomon wrote in the Song of Songs:

> King Solomon made himself a palanquin
> Of the wood of Lebanon . . .
> Go forth, O ye daughters of Zion,
> And gaze upon King Solomon
> Even upon the crown wherewith
> his mother has crowned him. . . .

Figure 22. Solomon on the alchemical throne, and Sheba arriving at its base. (Bibliothèque Nationale; lat. 512. *Speculum Humanae Salvationis*, fol. 11r.)

Again, he seems to feel that while his mother may have crowned him, he has made for himself his throne and is seated firmly upon it. His test of the Queen of Sheba is very important in this light, and she passes it with flying colors (S XXVII 42):

> So when she arrived,
> She was asked, "Is this
> Thy throne?" She said,
> "It was just like this;
> And knowledge was bestowed
> On us in advance of this,
> And we have submitted
> to God (in Islam)."

She recognizes that her throne has been altered, but it is still basically her own, and one senses she is affirming that it has been improved by her journey to Jerusalem. The concept of the throne as seat, power, knowledge, and symbol of authority is very important in Islam. One of the most healing and protective Suras of the Qur'an, the Throne or Kursi (S II 255) says:

> His Throne doth extend
> Over the heavens
> And the earth, and He feeleth
> No fatigue in guarding
> And preserving them
> For He is Most High,
> The Supreme (in glory).

The first major test passed, the Queen of Sheba is conducted to the palace where Solomon is seated on his throne which is placed on a glass floor. Some say this was done on advice of the djinn who told Solomon that the Queen of Sheba had hair on her legs, proving she was a demon. The ruse of the glass floor, with fish swimming beneath it, was intended to make the Queen raise her skirts, and reveal herself to Solomon. The Qur'an most vividly recounts this test (S XXVII 44):

> She was asked to enter
> The lofty Palace: but
> When she saw it, she
> Thought it was a lake
> Of water, and she (tucked up
> Her skirts), uncovering her legs.
> He said, "This is
> But a palace paved
> Smooth with slabs of glass."
> She said: "O my Lord!
> I have indeed wronged
> My soul: I do (now)
> Submit (in Islam), with Solomon,
> To the Lord of the Worlds."

And here is the second major test. The Queen of Sheba has responded to Solomon's gallantry and accepted his one God. She is one who is ready to be guided. Her heart is open. The second part of the testing, the riddles, seem to be a more personal and human exchange. They seem part of the King and Queen's getting to know each other, and their own natures as well.

Chapter 5

RIDDLE ME THIS, RIDDLE ME THAT

Solomon's tests of Sheba, the threatening letter, the shining Jehoiada, the throne on the glass sea, the stealing and disguising of her throne, are past. Sheba's tests of Solomon, her impressive gifts in response to his threats, her extraordinarily speedy arrival, her six thousand children born at the same moment, have only set the stage for the real knowing encounter of the two monarchs.

The use of riddles in folklore, fairy tales, Bible and myth is very familiar to us. The peculiarly differentiating, almost magical insight demonstrated by solving a riddle seems a credible reason for the great rewards bestowed upon the riddle solver. Indeed one who can solve a riddle seems to have divine inspiration. This archetype is behind the proliferation and development of the riddles asked of Solomon by Sheba in both Jewish

and Arabic folklore. God is believed to have given Solomon the ability to understand wisely, and Sheba is certainly seen to be seeking a connection to the one true
God in her questioning of Solomon. By asking riddles
the Queen of Sheba both brings wisdom and calls forth
wisdom.

> Or if you are eager for wide experience,
> She knows the past, She forecasts the future;
> She knows how to turn maxims and solve
>   riddles;
> She has foreknowledge of signs and wonders,
>   of the unfolding of the ages and the
>   stories (Wisdom 8:8).

While Solomon's tests of Sheba seem to have elements of challenge and competition, Sheba's riddles
posed to Solomon seem both more inviting and more
seductive. They have an almost wistful quality. She
seems to be hoping that he understands her and her
womanly nature, and, moreover, that his views about
spiritual and religious matters correspond to her own.
She needs to be seen by him. Perhaps she had heard of
his solution of the baby problem and she felt the differentiating sword of his wisdom cutting through to the
true mother's heart. Or perhaps she had experienced
the floor of glass as a mirror of her own problem, her
need, and had felt seen and known by him. Similarly,
Solomon's ability to move and transform her throne, to
know her power, must have made her feel known and
moved her, but still, she feels insecure, unsure, and

tests him with hard questions which become increasingly more personal for each of them.

She asks, at first: "Who is he who neither was born nor has died?" "It is the Lord of the world, blessed be He," answers Solomon. Then, to test his understanding of God's power as it is described in the Book, "What land is that which has but once seen the sun?" "The land upon which after creation the waters were gathered, and the bed of the Red Sea on the day when it was divided." Sheba, so identified with her own land, would of course, naturally, begin with this. Moreover, the Qur'an says that God had made the land of Sheba like the Garden of Eden, so she reminds Solomon of her own gifts in this way.

Then, there followed several riddles that seem designed to assure her that Solomon knows and understands the meaning of the Book, the Old Testament accounts of the golden calf, Jonah, Elijah, Samson, and Daniel, and that Solomon believes as she does — that life and death and all manner of miracles proceed from God. Now, the riddles become more subtle.

Sheba brought a number of men to Solomon, some circumcised and others uncircumcised, and asked him to distinguish between them. He immediately made a sign to the high priest, who opened the Ark of the Covenant. Those that were circumcised bowed their bodies to half their height while their countenances shone with the radiance of the Shekhina. The uncircumcised fell prone upon their faces. "Those," said Solomon, "are circumcised, those uncircumcised." Sheba understood from this answer that Solomon did indeed understand that only those who had opened their hearts to the one true God could bear the radiance of the Divine Presence, the feminine indwelling aspect of God.

Sheba then brought before Solomon a number of male and female youths dressed alike and of similar stature. She asked him to distinguish between the boys and the girls. He made a sign to the eunuchs who brought him a quantity of nuts and roasted ears of corn. These he spread before the youths. The males who were not bashful took them eagerly with their bare hands. The females, more veiled in their motives, took them more slowly, bringing their gloved hands from beneath their clothes. This may have been the first of Sheba's riddles specifically about feminine nature and processes. There followed a series of riddles, all regarding the facts of the soul.

She said, "Seven there are that issue, and nine that enter; two yield the draught, and one drinks." Said he to her, "Seven are the days of a woman's menstruation, and nine the months of pregnancy; two are the breasts that yield the draught, and one the child that drinks it." In a similar vein she asked, "There is an enclosure with ten doors, when one is open nine are shut; when nine are open, one is shut?" Said Solomon, "That enclosure is the womb; the ten doors are the ten orifices of man— his eyes, ears, nostrils, mouth, the apertures for the discharge of excreta and urine, and the navel. When the child is in the womb, the navel is open and the other orifices are closed, but when it issues from the womb, the navel is closed and the others are opened."

Then she questioned him further: "Three entered a cave and five came forth therefrom?" Solomon replied, "Lot and his two daughters and their two children." "A woman said to her son, your father is my father, and your grandfather my husband. You are my son and I am your sister." "Assuredly," said he, "It was the daughter of Lot who spoke this way to her son."

Then another question about this matter of incest: "A woman was wedded to two, and bore two sons, yet these four had one father. The answer Solomon gave was, "Tamar," who was married to Judah and to his father as well. The last question regarding the feminine mysteries was: "A cistern of wood, a bucket of iron. It draws up stones. They cause water to flow." Solomon's prompt reply; "A tube of kohl." These containers were often made of reeds and held a stick sometimes made of iron and finely powdered antimony stones. The stick was dipped into the kohl and then laid on the inner rim of the eye and the eyelid, causing tears to flow which outlined the eye in silvery black kohl.

Having ascertained that Solomon knew her mind regarding the nature of God and woman, Sheba began to question him about certain transformative alchemical processes: "Like dust it comes as from the earth. It is nourished from the dust of the earth. It is poured out like water, and illumines the house?" Solomon's answer: "Naptha." On the island of Napthonia in the Caspian Sea and other places in the East, naptha—or mineral oil—is a clear transparent material that flows from the earth where it is formed, and it is used for illumination.

And another: a storm wind rushes through their tops. It cries loudly and bitterly. Its head is like a rush. It is praiseworthy for the rich, shameworthy for the poor, honorable for the dead, disgraceful for the criminal, joyous for the birds, and grievous for the fish. The answer sought by Sheba is flax, which can be made into linen

Figure 23. The Queen of Sheba, by Edmund Dulac. *I would ask of Bilqis, and her ways, And her throne, red and gold intervein'd!* (Alquma ibn Dhu Jodon). *For ninety full years did Bilqis hold sway over her folk in all glory and might! Her massive throne eighty cubits each way with rubies and pearls and all jewels bedight!* (Ab-karib As'ad, King of Sheba, A.D. 275–425).

sails for ships which groan in the wind, clothes for the rich, which become rags for the poor, a shroud for the dead, a rope for the hanged, seed for birds and a net for fish.

Another process-oriented riddle is presented: Sheba ordered the sawn trunk of a cedar tree to be brought and she asked Solomon to point out at which end had been the root and at which had been the branches. He had the trunk cast into water. The root end sank; the branch end floated, as Solomon pointed out. Then Sheba said to him, "You exceed in wisdom and goodness the fame which I heard, blessed be your God!"

The Old Testament tells us that Sheba asked Solomon all that was in her heart and that he answered all that she did ask. Then there was no breath left in her!

And she said to the king: "It was a true report that I heard in mine own land of thine acts, and of thy wisdom. Howbeit I believed not the words, until I came, and mine own eyes had seen it; and, behold, the half was not told me; thou hast wisdom and prosperity exceeding the fame which I heard" (I Kings 10:6-8)!

The Queen of Sheba has indeed had a healing *experience*. She understands now that received ideas are merely opinion, notions, nothing compared to knowledge of the heart based on one's own experience, and she concludes, "Blessed be the Lord thy God, who delighted in thee, to set thee on the throne of Israel." So, we see that from Sheba's point of view it is God that has set Solomon on his throne and given him wisdom and understanding. The Bible says that she then gave Solomon much gold and precious stones, and an abundance of spices never seen before (figure 23, page 86). Among the never seen before healing balms were balsam, and it is believed that the precious stone she gave to him was the philosopher's stone, the treasure hard to attain. "And King Solomon gave to the Queen of Sheba all her desire, whatsoever she asked, beside that which Solomon gave her of her royal bounty" (I Kings 10:13).

Chapter 6

THE CONIUNCTIO – THE KNOWING CONNECTION

T he tests Solomon had made of Sheba and questions Sheba had asked of Solomon resulted in the following exchange. The Queen spoke unto King Solomon, saying:

> "O how greatly have pleased me thy answering, and the sweetness of thy voice, and the beauty of thy going, and the graciousness of thy words, and the readiness thereof. The sweetness of thy voice maketh the heart to rejoice, and maketh the bones fat, and giveth courage to hearts, and goodwill and grace to the lips, and

strength to the gait. I look upon thee and I see that thy wisdom is immeasurable and thine understanding inexhaustible, and that it is like unto a lamp in the darkness, and like unto a pomegranate in the garden, and like unto a pearl in the sea, and like unto the Morning Star among the stars, and like unto the light of the Moon in the mist, and like unto a glorious dawn and sunrise in the heavens. And I give thanks unto Him that brought me hither and showed thee to me, and made me to tread upon the threshold of thy gate, and made me to hear thy voice."

And King Solomon answered and said unto her, "Wisdom and understanding spring from thee thyself. As for me, I only possess them in the measure in which the God of ISRAEL hath given them to me because I asked and entreated them from Him. And thou, although thou dost not know the God of ISRAEL, hast this wisdom which thou hast made to grow in thine heart, and it hath made thee come to see me" (Kebra Nagast 26).

There has been a meeting, an exchange of trust and understanding, and a knowing connection made between these two people (see figure 24 on page 91). Each has seen and felt the wisdom of the other and each feels grateful to God for their meeting. The Queen of Sheba, in each of the holy books, the Bible, the Qur'an and the Kebra Nagast, renounces her previous Sun and Moon worship and accepts the one God of Solomon,

CONIVNCTIO SIVE
Coitus.

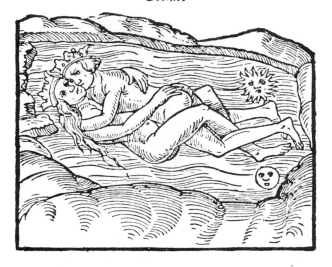

Figure 24. *O Moon, folded in my embrace, Be you strong as I, as fair of face! O Sun, brightest of all lights known to men, And yet you need me, as the cock and the hen.* This alchemical drawing shows the Coniunctio, an ancient image that continues to be meaningful today.

the Creator of the Universe. The Queen of Sheba asked Solomon:

> "Tell me now: whom is it right for me to wor-
> ship? We worship the sun according as our

fathers have taught us to do, because we say that the sun is the king of the gods. And there are others among our subjects who worship other things; some worship stones, and some worship wood [i.e., trees], and some worship carved figures, and some worship images of gold and silver. And we worship the sun, for he cooketh our food, and moreover, he illumineth the darkness, and removeth fear; we call him 'Our King,' and we call him 'Our Creator,' and we worship him as our god; for no man hath told us that besides him there is another god. But we have heard that there is with you, ISRAEL, another God Whom we do not know, and men have told us that He hath sent down to you from heaven a Tabernacle and hath given unto you a Tablet of the ordering of the angels, by the hand of MOSES the Prophet. This also we have heard—that He Himself cometh down to you and talketh to you, and informeth you concerning His ordinances and commandments" (Kebra Nagast 27).

And the King answered and said unto her, "Verily, it is right that they [i.e., men] should worship God, Who created the universe, the heavens and the earth, the sea and the dry land, the sun and the moon, the stars and the brilliant bodies of the heavens, the trees and the stones, the beasts and the feathered fowl, the wild beasts and the crocodiles, the fish and the whales, the hippopotamuses and the water lizards, the lightnings and the crashes of thunder,

the clouds and the thunders, and the good and
the evil. It is meet that Him alone we should
worship, in fear and trembling, with joy and
with gladness. For He is the Lord of the Universe, the Creator of angels and men. And it is
He Who killeth and maketh to live, it is He Who
inflicteth punishment and showeth compassion, Who raiseth up from the ground him that
is in misery, Who exalteth the poor from the
dust, Who maketh to be sorrowful and Who
maketh to rejoice, Who raiseth up and Who
bringeth down. No one can chide Him, for He is
the Lord of the Universe, and there is no one
who can say unto Him, 'What hast Thou done?'
And unto Him it is meet that there should be
praise and thanksgiving from angels and men.
And as concerning what thou sayest, that 'He
hath given unto you the Tabernacle of the Law,'
verily there hath been given unto us the Tabernacle of the God of ISRAEL, which was created
before all creation by His glorious counsel. And
He hath made to come down to us His commandments, done into writing, so that we may
know His decree and the judgement that He
hath ordained in the mountain of His
holiness."

And the Queen said,"From this moment I will
not worship the sun, but will worship the Creator of the sun, the God of ISRAEL. And that
Tabernacle of the god of ISRAEL shall be unto
me my Lady, and unto my seed after me, and
unto all my kingdoms that are under my domin-

ion. And because of this I have found favour
before thee, and before the God of ISRAEL my
Creator, Who hath brought me unto thee, and
hath made me to hear thy voice, and hath
shown me thy face, and hath made me to
understand thy commandment" (Kebra Nagast
28).

After having dwelt in the land of Solomon for six
months the Queen of Sheba told Solomon that she
wished to return to her own land:

And when the Queen sent her message to
SOLOMON, saying that she was about to
depart to her own country, he pondered in his
heart and said, "A woman of such splendid
beauty hath come to me from the ends of the
earth! What do I know? Will God give me seed
in her?" Now, as it is said in the Book of Kings,
SOLOMON the King was a lover of women.
And he married wives of the HEBREWS, and
the EGYPTIANS, and the CANAANITES, and
the EDOMITES, and the MOABITES, and from
SYRIA, and women who were reported to be
beautiful. And he had four hundred queens and
six hundred concubines. Now this which he did
was not for the sake of fornication, but as a
result of the wise intent that God had given
unto him.

And SOLOMON said in his heart, "What do I
know? Peradventure God will give me men
children from each one of these women." There-

fore when he did thus he acted wisely, saying, "My children shall inherit the cities of the enemy, and shall destroy those who worship idols."

So Solomon formulated a plan:

King SOLOMON sent a message unto the Queen, saying, "Now that thou hast come here why wilt thou go away without seeing the administration of the kingdom, and how the meals for the chosen ones of the kingdom are eaten after the manner of the righteous . . .? From the sight of it thou wouldst acquire wisdom. Follow me now and seat thyself in my splendour in the tent, and I will complete thy instruction, and thou shalt learn the administration of my kingdom; for thou hast loved wisdom, and she shall dwell with thee until thine end and for ever." Now a prophecy maketh itself apparent in this speech.

And the Queen sent a second message, saying, "From being a fool, I have become wise by following thy wisdom, and from being a thing rejected by the God of ISRAEL, I have become a chosen woman because of this faith which is in my heart; and henceforth I will worship no other god except Him. And as concerning that which thou sayest, that thou wishest to increase in me wisdom and honour, I will come according to thy desire." And SOLOMON rejoiced because of this message (Kebra Nagast 29).

Figure 25. This painting on leather is a recent rendition of a traditional Ethiopian painting of Solomon and Sheba at the feast he gave for her before their "wedding." (From the author's collection.)

He made his tent ready for her visit:

> He beautified the place where she would be
> seated, and had spread over it purple hangings,
> and laid down carpets, and decorated it with
> marble and precious stones, and he burned aro-
> matic powders, and sprinkled oil of myrrh and
> cassia round about, and scattered frankincense
> and costly incense in all directions. And when
> they brought her into this abode, the odour
> thereof was very pleasing to her, and even
> before she ate the dainty meats therein she was
> satisfied with the smell of them. And with wise
> intent SOLOMON sent to her meats which
> would make her thirsty, and drinks that were
> mingled with vinegar, and fish and dishes made
> with pepper. And this he did and he gave them
> to the Queen to eat. And the royal meal had
> come to an end three courses and seven courses
> had been served, and the administrators, and
> the counsellors, and the young men and the
> servants had departed, and the King rose up
> and he went to the Queen, and he said to her—
> now they were alone together—"Take thou
> thine ease here for love's sake until daybreak."
> And she said unto him, "Swear to me by thy
> God, the God of ISRAEL, that thou wilt not
> take me by force. For if I, who according to the
> law of men am a maiden, be seduced, I should
> travel on my journey home in sorrow, and
> affliction, and tribulation" (Kebra Nagast 29).

And SOLOMON answered and said unto her, "I swear unto thee that I will not take thee by force, but thou must swear unto me that thou wilt not take by force anything that is in my house." And the Queen laughed and said unto him, "Being a wise man why dost thou speak as a fool? Shall I steal anything, or shall I carry out of the house of the King that which the King hath not given to me? Do not imagine that I have come hither through love of riches. Moreover, my own kingdom is as wealthy as thine, and there is nothing which I wish for that I lack. Assuredly I have only come in quest of thy wisdom." And he said unto her, "If thou wouldst make me swear, swear thou to me, for a swearing is meet for both of us, so that neither of us may be unjustly treated. And if thou wilt not make me swear I will not make thee swear." And she said unto him, "Swear to me that thou wilt not take me by force, and I on my part will swear not to take by force thy possessions"; and he swore to her and made her swear.

And the King went up on his bed on the one side of the chamber, and the servants made ready for her a bed on the other side. And SOLOMON said unto a young manservant, "Wash out the bowl and set in it a vessel of water whilst the Queen is looking on, and shut the doors and go and sleep." And SOLOMON spake to the servant in another tongue which the Queen did not understand, and he did as the King commanded, and went and slept. And

the King had not as yet fallen asleep, but he
only pretended to be asleep, and he was watch-
ing the Queen intently. Now the house of
SOLOMON the King was illumined as by day,
for in his wisdom he had made shining pearls
which were like unto the sun, and moon, and
stars and had set them in the roof of his house.

And the Queen slept a little. And when she
woke up her mouth was dry with thirst, for the
food which SOLOMON had given her in his
wisdom had made her thirsty, and she was very
thirsty indeed, and her mouth was dry; and she
moved her lips and sucked with her mouth and
found no moisture. And she determined to
drink the water which she had seen, and she
looked at King SOLOMON and watched him
carefully, and she thought that he was sleeping
a sound sleep. But he was not asleep, and he
was waiting until she should rise up to steal the
water to quench her thirst. And she rose up
and, making no sound with her feet, she went
to the water in the bowl and lifted up the jar to
drink the water. And SOLOMON seized her
hand before she could drink the water, and said
unto her, "Why hast thou broken the oath that
thou hast sworn that thou wouldst not take by
force anything that is in my house?" And she
answered and said unto him in fear, "Is the oath
broken by my drinking water?" And the King
said unto her, "Is there anything that thou hast
seen under the heavens that is better than
water?" And the Queen said, "I have sinned

Figure 26. Ethiopian painting of the arrival of the Queen of Sheba in Jerusalem and King Solomon entertaining her (Chronique du regne de Menelik II by Guebre Sellassie, Paris, 1930, School of Oriental and African Studies, London).

against myself, and thou art free from thy oath.
But let me drink water for my thirst." Then
SOLOMON said unto her, "Am I perchance
free from the oath which thou hast made me
swear?" And the Queen said, "Be free from thy
oath, only let me drink water." And he permit-
ted her to drink water, and after she had drunk
water he worked his will with her and they
slept together (Kebra Nagast 30).

Although this elaborate story of an actual physical
coniunctio between Solomon and Sheba is told in the
Kebra Nagast (see figure 26 and 27, pp. 100 and 102),
both Jewish and Arabic folklore also support the theme.
The Hebrew verb *ben'*, usually translated as "she came
to Solomon" generally means "to come in." In more
than a dozen places in the Bible it is used specifically for
entering a tent or a house for purposes of sexual relations. It is used this way in the story of the daughters of
Lot "going in" to their father (Gen. 19:34). Two of Sheba's riddles concern these incestuous relations. In addi-
tion the phrase "He gave her all that she desired" (I
Kings 13) is often romantically interpreted to mean that
Sheba desired to make love with Solomon and to bear
his child.

There is also in Jewish folklore an identification of
Sheba with Lilith, the sexually tempting demon. Both
are supposed to have had hairy legs, characteristic of a
demonic instinctual nature — Sheba's being revealed by
the glass floor of Solomon's throne room. Solomon is
said to have wished to lie with Sheba even then, but to
have found her hairiness unattractive. A witch warned
him that Sheba's hairy legs proved she was a donkey-

Figure 27. Detail of a traditional Ethiopian representation of the Solomon and Sheba story. Top, left to right: Sheba sets out to visit Solomon; they meet. Bottom: Solomon seizes her; then they sleep together. (Picture courtesy of Ethiopian Airlines.)

legged woman! Arabic and Jewish folklore holds that
Solomon sent the Queen of Sheba a depilatory cream
called *nurah*, made of strychnine and slaked lime. Fur-
thermore, the Arabic name for Sheba is Bilqis, which
may be derived from the Hebrew word *pilgish*, meaning
prostitute. The Ethiopian name for Sheba is Makeda,
which means "woman of fire," also suggesting that it
was she who passionately desired and tempted Solomon. Medieval alchemists saw Solomon as the principle
who stood in fiery emotion (see figure 28, p. 104) and
was known to love many women.

Here is the alchemical coniunctio of equal opposites: King and Queen, Sol and Luna, He and She, and
in this union of the two something is needed by each,
and something is given by each to the other; that which
is wounded is healed, that which is burdened is freed,
and that which was lost is found. There is an exchange
of essences, and a feeling of completion and
blessedness.

Whether Sheba seduced Solomon, or Solomon
seduced Sheba, there remains the seemingly incontro-
vertible fact of a sexual union between the two,
resulting—according to the Ethiopian tradition at least—
in the conception and birth of a child called Menyelek,
son of the wise man. The Old Testament quotes Sheba
as saying to Solomon, "Happy are thy wives," and in
the Kebra Nagast, she wishes that she could be as one
of his lowly handmaidens, and wash his feet, as Mary
Magdalene would later wash the feet of Jesus, and dry
them with her hair. She finds King Solomon to be very
handsome. She loves the sweet sound of his voice, and

Figure 28. The coniunctio as a meeting of king and queen. The queen stands on a globe to indicate her connection with the Earth; the king stands in fire, showing the emotional attraction. (From Trismosin, *Splendor Solis*, MS 1582, British Museum.)

she says that it "maketh the heart to rejoice and maketh the bones fat." Solomon for his part goes to great lengths to engage her equally, as he needs her to be, and to make love to her. He is certainly attracted to her beauty and intelligence, and sometimes frightened of her equalness. She is equal to him in strength and in need. (See figure 24, page 91.)

After Solomon and Sheba had made love to each other, and slept together:

> There appeared unto King SOLOMON in a dream a brilliant sun, and it came down from heaven and shed exceedingly great splendour over ISRAEL. And when it had tarried there for a time it suddenly withdrew itself, and it flew away to the country of Sheba, and it shone there with exceedingly great brightness for ever, for it willed to dwell there. And the King said, "I waited to see if it would come back to ISRAEL, but it did not return."

> "And again while I waited a light rose up in the heavens and a sun came down from them in the land of Judah and it sent forth light that was very much stronger than before" (Kebra Nagast 30).

This dream from the Kebra Nagast seems to echo the fear and alarm expressed by Solomon in the Song of Songs (3:6–7):

> What is this coming up from the desert
> like a column of smoke,
> breathing of myrrh and frankincense
> and every perfume the merchant knows?

Solomon continues; trying to reassure himself he says, "Behold, it is the litter of Solomon, surrounded by three score mighty warriors. Each man has his sword at his side, against alarms at night" (Song of Songs 3:7–8).

In the midst of a song that begins, "How beautiful you are, my love, how beautiful you are!" (Song of Songs 4:1–2), he suddenly, after saying ". . . your words are enchanting . . ." again shows fear of his beautiful lover:

> Your neck is the tower of David
> built as a fortress,
> hung round with a thousand bucklers
> and each the shield of a hero (Song of Songs 4:4–5).

In a later song he asks:

> Who is this arising like the dawn,
> fair as the moon
> resplendent as the sun
> terrible as an army with banners? (Song of Songs 6:10–11)

So we see how Solomon had sensed intuitively, as Sheba approached, that her power would rise, and the Sun would pass from his glorious realm to hers. The Zohar (II 249a–250a), the Book of Splendor of the Qabalists, says that when David gave the kingdom to Solomon it was whole, but that because of Solomon's excesses with women, the Kingdom of Israel declined, like the waning Moon. Thus, the dream Solomon has after making love to Sheba confirms his worst fears. The Kebra Nagast continues:

> And when SOLOMON the King saw this vision in his sleep, his soul became disturbed, and his understanding was snatched away as by a flash of lightning, and he woke up with an agitated mind. And moreover, SOLOMON marvelled concerning the Queen, for she was vigorous in strength, and beautiful of form, and she was undefiled in her virginity; and she had reigned for six years in her own country, and, notwithstanding her gracious attraction and her splendid form, had preserved her body pure.

So Sheba has remained true to herself, whole and beautiful.

> And the Queen said unto SOLOMON, "Dismiss me, and let me depart to my own country." And he went into his house and gave unto her whatsoever she wished for of splendid things and riches, and beautiful apparel which bewitched the eyes, and everything on which great store was set in the country of ETHIOPIA, and camels and wagons, six thousand in number, which were laden with beautiful things of the most desirable kind, and wagons wherein loads were carried over the desert, and a vessel wherein one could travel over the sea, and a vessel wherein one could traverse the air (or winds), which SOLOMON had made by the

wisdom that God had given unto him (Kebra
Nagast 30).

And the Queen rejoiced, and she went forth in
order to depart, and the King set her on her way
with great pomp and ceremony. And SOLO-
MON took her aside so that they might be alone
together, and he took off the ring that was upon
his little finger, and he gave it to the Queen, and
said unto her, "Take this so that thou mayest
not forget me. And if it happen that I obtain
seed from thee, this ring shall be unto it a sign;
and if it be a man child he shall come to me; and
the peace of God be with thee! Whilst I was
sleeping with thee I saw many visions in a
dream, and it seemed as if a sun had risen upon
Israel, but it snatched itself away and flew off
and lighted up the country of Sheba; peradventure that country shall be blessed through thee;
God knoweth. And as for thee, observe what I
have told thee, so that thou mayest worship
God with all thy heart and perform His Will.
For He punisheth those who are arrogant, and
He showeth compassion upon those who are
humble, and He removeth the thrones of the
mighty, and He maketh to be honoured those
who are needy. For death and life are from Him,
and riches and poverty are bestowed by His
Will. For everything is His, and none can
oppose His command and His judgement in the
heavens, or in the earth, or in the sea, or in the
abysses. And may God be with thee! Go in

peace." And they separated from each other (Kebra Nagast).

Nine months and five days after she had separated from King Solomon, the Queen of Sheba gave birth to a man child whom she called Ben l'hakim, which means, son of the wise man. The Kebra Nagast continues the story, telling that when Bayna-Lehkem grew up he returned to Jerusalem, met his father who recognized him immediately even before Bayna-Lehkem showed him the ring that Solomon had given Sheba. Eventually, Bayna-Lehkem, the son of Solomon and Sheba, carried the Ark of the Covenant away from Israel to the Land of Sheba. Another strand of Qabalistic folklore holds that their son was Nebuchadnezzer who also spelled destruction for the Jews.

Solomon's glory declined as his dream had predicted. In his later Biblical writing he seems bitter and disappointed. The Kebra Nagast is even more explicit. Solomon cried out:

> "Woe is me! Woe is me! I weep for myself. Rise up, DAVID, my father, and weep with me for our Lady, for God hath neglected us and hath taken away our Lady from thy son. Woe is me! Woe is me! Woe is me! For the Sun of righteousness hath neglected me. Woe is me! For we have neglected the command of our God, and we have become rejected ones on the earth" (Kebra Nagast 60).

Chapter 7

KING SOLOMON'S DECLINE

The Bible, which is so rich in detail of Solomon's wisdom, his buildings, his treasures, his administration and realm, is silent about his death. It says only that he slept with his fathers. It does not say whether he persisted in worshipping strange gods and goddesses and idols or whether he returned to the one God. Some rabbinic writers say that Solomon asked God to conceal his death so that some of his unfinished works would be completed by the djinns and demons who worked for him. Accordingly, as Solomon felt his strength failing, he remained on his knees in prayer leaning on his staff, and the demons, believing him to be alive, continued their work. The Qur'an adds that a crawling reptile was the first to learn of Solomon's death and gnawed the staff that supported the corpse. When it collapsed, the demons stopped working. The Zohar, the Qabalist's *Book of Splendor*, says,

Now, we have a tradition that Solomon was wont to rise each day at daybreak and turn his face towards the east, where he saw certain things—and then toward the south, where also he saw certain things, and finally, to the side of the north. He would stand thus with his head raised and his eyes half-closed until there would come towards him two pillars, one of fire and one of cloud, and borne upon this last an eagle, mighty in stature and strength, his right wing resting upon the fire, and his body and left wing upon the cloud. This eagle bore in his mouth two leaves. The pillar of cloud with the two leaves and the pillar of fire and the eagle upon them, would come and bow before Solomon. Then the eagle would bend down its head a little, and give him the leaves. Solomon would take and smell them, and by their odour could discern from whence they came, and recognize one leaf as belonging to him "who has his eyes shut," and the other to him "who has his eyes open" (cf. Num. xxv, 4). Now there were a number of things which King Solomon desired that these two beings should make known to him. What did he do? He sealed up his throne with a ring on which was engraved the Holy Name, drew forth from a hidden place another

ring on which the Holy Name was also
engraved, ascended unto the roof of his palace,
seated himself upon the eagle's back, and so
departed, attended both by fire and cloud. The
eagle ascended into the heavens, and wherever
he passed the earth below was darkened. The
wiser sort in that part of the earth from whence
the light was thus suddenly removed would
know the cause and would say, "Assuredly that
was King Solomon passing by!" but they knew
not whither he went. The vulgar sort, however,
would say, "Up there the clouds are moving,
and that is why it grew dark so suddenly." The
eagle would mount up even to the height of
four hundred parasangs, until it reached at
length the dark mountain, where is Tarmud in
the wilderness; and there at last it would
descend. Solomon would then lift up his head
and see the dark mountain, and would learn
therefrom all that it could teach him and also
perceive that it was necessary to penetrate further; after which he would mount once more
the back of the eagle and fly on as before until
they entered into the depths of the mountains,
in the midst of which grew an olive tree. When
he was arrived at this spot Solomon would cry
out with all his might: "Lord, thy hand is lifted
up, they see not" (Is. xxvi, 11). Then he would
enter that place until he reached those who
abode there, and he would show them his ring,
and there he gained all his knowledge of
strange sciences, i.e., witchcraft. When they
had told him all that he required he would fly

back to his palace in the same way that he came. Then, as he sat once more on his throne, he would reflect upon all that he had gone through, and would conceive ideas of profound wisdom (Zohar III 112b–113a).

In another passage of the Zohar (V 194 a–b):

We have found in the Book of Asmodai which he gave to King Solomon, that anyone who desires to make powerful enchantments, if he knows the rock where Balaam fell, will find there snakes formed from the bones of that wicked one, and if he kills one he can make certain enchantments with its head and others with its body, and others again with its tail, there being three kinds in each one. One of the questions which the Queen of Sheba asked Solomon was how to take hold of the bone of the serpent of three enchantments. . . . These are secret mysteries which should not be revealed, only in order that the Companions here should know the hidden ways of the world I have revealed them.

During the Middle Ages, a tradition arose that Solomon had died in sin, authored a book of sorcery and magic called *Clavicules de Solomon* and had commerce with demons. (See figure 29.)

There are many versions of this book. Sometimes it is called the book of Raziel and sometimes, in the Zohar, it is known as the book that Asmodai the devil gave Solomon. There exist a plethora of magic circles called

Figure 29. The Demon Belial presents his credentials to Solomon. (Jacobus de Teramo, *Das Buch Belial*, Augsburg, 1473.)

the Seal of Solomon, and many elaborate instructions for drawing such a circle and for its use (see figures 30 and 31, p. 116 and 117). The circles usually contain the magic names of God. The magical properties are evoked through the use of words, daggers, crystals, candles and incantations. Solomon himself confesses all his sins in the Kebra Nagast:

> "Of our own free will we have polluted our life. Woe be unto us! Woe be unto us! The repentance and mercy which God loveth we have not done. Woe be unto us! He gave us glory, and we have thrown it away. He made us very wise,

Figure 30. The magic circle and the accessories for evocation (from Barrett: *The Magus*, 1801).

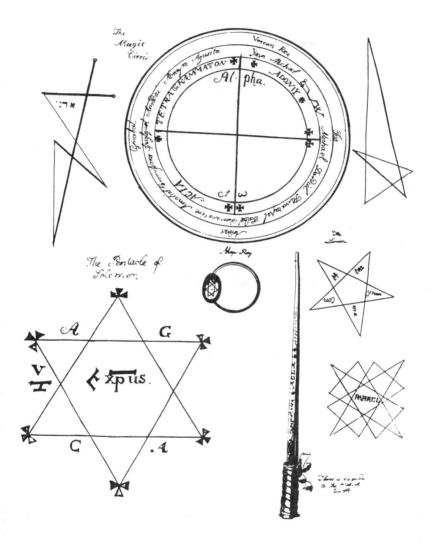

Figure 31. A magic circle, ring, and pentacle attributed to Solomon (from Barrett: *The Magus*, 1801).

and of our own free will we have made ourselves more foolish than the beasts. He gave us riches, and we have beggared ourselves even to asking for alms. We looked upon our horses, and forgot our coming back. We have loved fleeting things, and we have not recognized those that abide. We have made our days to deride our life, we have preferred the luxuriousness of food, which becometh dung, to the food of life which endureth for ever. We have put on the garments of apparel which benefit not the soul, and have put off the apparel of glory which is for ever. Our governors and the people do what God hateth, and they love not what God loveth, love of their neighbours, and lowliness, and graciousness, and mercy for the poor, and patient endurance, and love of the house of God, and the adoration of the Son. But what God hateth is, augury by birds, and idolatry, and enquiry of witches, and divination, and magic, and flies, and the animal that hath been torn, and the dead body of a beast, and theft, and oppression, and fornication, and envy, fraud, drink and drunkenness, false swearing against neighbours, and the bearing of false testimony against neighbours."

All the holy books agree: Solomon was led astray by his attraction to beautiful exotic women who turned his heart away from the God of his fathers and toward their own gods and idolatry.

> For it came to pass, when
> Solomon was old that his wives
> turned away his heart after other gods;
> and his heart was not whole with the
> Lord his God, as was the heart of David
> his father (I Kings 11:4–5).

God became angry with Solomon and determined to wrest the kingdom from him, leaving only one tribe to Solomon's son, Rehoboam, "for the sake of David" (I Kings 11:9–13).

Thus, while the coniunctio between Solomon and Sheba left Sheba full of a new conception, secure in her love of wisdom and God, Solomon was relatively unchanged. He had given his seed, but not his heart. His dream bespeaks the Sol Niger, the darkening and depression of a man in the second half of life unable to regenerate himself because of a defect of heart, a tendency to go from woman to woman, always projecting his anima and unable to develop a feeling connection, and so overly identified with consciousness, solar logic, rationalization, dark magic, power, and self-justification that he has no shadow, and no depth. Because the Sun is no longer personally his own, Solomon hates it and cannot bear it.

The Zohar says that when David was king he was in a good relation to God. He sang praises to God from below, thus seeking wealth and completeness.

> When the moon is full it is called "the field of apples," but when it is defective it is called "the field of poverty." Hence, praise from below affords it wealth and completeness, and so

David all his lifetime sought to provide this completeness by chanting hymns of praise below. When David died he left it complete, and Solomon received it at its full, since the moon had escaped from poverty and entered into riches. By means of these riches Solomon ruled over all the kings of the earth, and therefore "silver was not accounted for anything in the days of Solomon" (I Kings 10:21), but everything was of gold. . . .

But, Solomon had no need to sing like David, save one song which is beloved of wealth, and is the jewel and favourite of all chants of praises, since it contains the praises recited by the Matron when she sits on the throne opposite the King. Everything was gold, and dust was joined with the left hand, on the side of love, and the sun clung to it and did not part from it. Solomon was hereby led into error. He saw that the moon had approached the sun and the right hand was embracing and the left hand under the head. Seeing this he said: "What need is there of the right hand here, seeing that they have drawn near to one another?" God then said to him: "I swear to thee that as thou hast rejected the right hand, thou shalt one day require the kindness that comes from the right side of men and shalt not obtain it." Straight away the sun parted from the moon, and the moon began to darken, and Solomon went begging and said: "I am Koheleth," and no one would show him kindness (Zohar II 249b–250a).

Solomon's rejection of the right hand, *chesed*, loving kindness, submission to God, and his overvaluing of idolatry, magic, power, wealth, and despotism brings about his downfall. The Zohar (IV 216a) expresses it well:

> After fear comes love. This is esoterically expressed by saying: "After fear has hovered over a man's head there awakens love, which belongs to the right side." For he who worships out of love attaches himself to a very sublime region and to the holiness of the "World-to-be," by reason of love ascending to the "right side" for its attachment and adornment.

Solomon had no fear of God, and thus no real love of God. He overvalued his own gifts and, in his old age, the loving of foreign women who turned his heart away from God so that he died a besotted, effeminate, embittered despot.

Chapter 8

THE SONG OF AURORA DAWN

While Solomon declined, Sheba, because of her essentially feminine lunar nature—sometimes dark and sometimes light—was able to integrate and hold the opposites within herself. Moreover, once it was pierced by the love of wisdom, her questing heart led her, and she trusted her Self. In describing this con-iunctio, the alchemist Philalethes writes, "The Royal Diadem appears in the menstruum of a whore."[1] Smitten with love of wisdom, wisdom as mother, sister, and wise man, the Queen of Sheba was an explorer at heart. Seeking her own experience in place of received ideas,

---

[1] Philalethes, "Introitus apertus," *Musaem Hermeticum*, Frankfurt, 1678, p. 654.

she went to Jerusalem to see Solomon and fell in love with God.

Medieval Christian mystics speak of the Queen of Sheba as a prophetess or seer because of her role in the legend of the True Cross. It is said that when Adam lay dying, his son Seth traveled to the Garden of Eden to buy a few drops of oil from the Tree of Mercy. Instead, the Archangel Michael gave Seth a branch of the Tree of Knowledge. Seth returned to find that Adam had died. He planted the branch of the Tree over his father's grave. In time it grew into a mighty tree. Centuries later Solomon cut it down to use for building the Temple and his workmen found that it absolutely refused to meet construction requirements, being at times too short, and at other times, too long. Thereupon, they became impatient and threw the tree across a pond to act as a bridge. When the Queen of Sheba came to test Solomon with hard questions she had to cross the pond and had a vision that the Savior would one day hang upon this tree. Therefore, she refused to put her foot on it. Instead she raised her skirts, as in the Quranic story, and waded across the pond. In some of these tales of Sheba and the True Cross, it is said that her wounded or animal foot is healed.

So we see again, that Solomon—his ego identified with the outer world of doing—repeatedly tries to gain what he needs from sexual congress with women. He commands, controls, connives, and, eventually, declines. Sheba, as a questing ego, sees, senses and follows her inner vision. She walks barefoot through it and has a true experience. She does not stay ensconced in her own old, conservative, contained, powerful position. She changes, and is thus transformed and healed. (See figure 32, p. 126.)

In Solomon's realm, where one might say the doing, making, achieving ego is King, there can arise an overweening power-drive. There is a confusion of ego and Self, and one becomes identified with what one does, and feels that one has nothing for oneself. Thus, the person seeks out relationships, looks for love, someone else to love one's Self. Solomon does this, and ultimately, inevitably, fails.

Sheba is Queen of a land that is already made. She worships Sun, Moon, and planets. There they do less, and submit more. She lives in harmony with nature, but she, too, becomes overly identified with her ego position of simply being. Suddenly, she is pierced by love. She is summoned by Solomon's need, and her own love of wisdom.

The experience of falling in love is always felt to be an expression of God's will—often a blessed, miraculous, falling, submission—but certainly it is never merely the ego's idea. Even the most adamant atheist experiences love as something more, something "other."

There is a mystery here. Like Sheba, who arrives at Solomon's throne full of questions, a woman who was newly, suddenly, deeply, profoundly in love dreamed that she sat opposite her lover. He had been transformed into a woman called Amber Woman, who would not speak except to reveal that her name was Melusina. Jung writes of Melusina:

Figure 32. Sheba crosses the water and is healed. (From the Dutch Geschiedenis van het heylighe Cruys, 1483, British Museum.)

Now this figure is certainly not an allegorical chimera or a mere metaphor: she has her particular psychic reality in that she is a glamorous apparition who by her very nature is on one side a psychic vision but also, on account of the psyche's capacity for imaginative realization (which Paracelsus calls Ares), is a distinct objective entity, like a dream which temporarily becomes reality. The figure of Melusina is eminently suited to this purpose. The anima belongs to those borderline phenomena which chiefly occur in special psychic situations. They are characterized by the more or less sudden collapse of a form or style of life which till then seemed the indispensable foundation of the individual's whole career. When such a catastrophe occurs, not only are all bridges back into the past broken, but there seems to be no way forward into the future. One is confronted with a hopeless and impenetrable darkness, an abysmal void that is now suddenly filled with an alluring vision, the palpably real presence of a strange yet helpful being, in the same way that, when one lives for a long time in great solitude, the silence or the darkness becomes visibly, audibly, and tangibly alive, and the unknown in oneself steps up in an unknown guise.[2]

---

[2]C. G. Jung, *Alchemical Studies*, Bollingen Series XX, Volume 13 of the Collected Works, Tr. by R. F. C. Hull (Princeton, NJ: Princeton University Press, 1967), § 216.

This is the time in a love affair where one tends to project the miraculous, healing, precious feeling onto the beloved. So, in the Song of Songs we have:

Let him kiss me with the kisses of his mouth.
Your love is more delightful than wine;
delicate is the fragrance of your perfume,
your name is an oil poured out. . . . (I:1–3)

This is the time in a relationship where one finds one-self speaking the lover's name all the time. She continues

. . . how right it is to love you . . .
I am black but comely . . . (I:4–5)

While the King rests in his own room
    my nard yields its perfume.
My beloved is a sachet of myrrh
    lying between my breasts . . . (I:12–13)

How beautiful you are, my love
    how beautiful you are!
All green is our bed. (I:15–16)

He has taken me to his banquet hall,
    and the banner he raises over me is love,
Feed me with raisin cakes,
    restore me with apples,
    for I am sick with love. (II:4–6)

The Song of Songs continues with more and more exaltation and idealization given to the lover and then, occasionally more and more flickers of loss:

> On my bed at night, I sought him
>> whom my heart loves,
> I sought but did not find him. (III:1-3)

Here is the beginning of the opening to Self knowledge. The Song continues, with reunions and projections.

> Your eyes, behind your veil, are doves;
> Your hair is like a flock of goats
>> frisking down the slopes of Gilead.
>> (IV:1-2)

> Your two breasts are two fawns,
>> twins of a gazelle,
>> that feed among the lilies. (IV:5-6)

But, inevitably, when lovers project all their feelings onto each other, as indeed they must, there is the sense of loss:

> I sleep but my heart is awake.
> I hear my Beloved knocking
> "Open to me, my sister, my love, ..."

The woman wonders:

> I have taken off my tunic,
> am I to put it on again?
> I have washed my feet,
> am I to dirty them again?
>
> My beloved thrust his hand
> through the hole in the door.
> I trembled to the core of my being.
> Then I rose
>   to open to my Beloved,
> myrrh ran off my hands,
> pure myrrh ran off my fingers
> onto the handles of the bolt.
>
> I opened to my beloved
> but he had turned his back and gone!
> My soul failed at his flight.
> I sought him but I did not find him.
> I called to him but he did not answer. (V:2–6)

Here is the terrible sense of loss where one must begin to take back inside, into oneself, the projections one has put upon the other. Here begins the painful, arduous work of the real inner marriage. For Solomon, it comes with the dream of the Sun leaving him when Sheba departs. Sheba carries the soul's transformation. She carries the new conception, the new birth, and the new age. Thus, she sees it and the New Testament Gospels of Matthew and Luke say, "Behold, something greater than Solomon *is* here." Perhaps because the Queen of Sheba has made the full journey, undertaking the experience that her heart and vision required of her—worshipped God as *Haqq*, truth, and reality—she becomes individuated.

The woman who had dreamt of her lover as Amber Woman or Melusina who had climbed the tree of Wisdom (see figure 33 on page 132) dreamt at the end of her love affair, "God will provide all you want and need." She had seen the truth. Her lover, because of his human limitations, was not able to give her all she wanted and needed, but God, or the Self, would provide.

In the Gospel of St. Matthew (12:42), and again in Luke (11:31), when people of an evil and adulterous generation who are acting out, acting badly, and godless, are asking for a sign, the gospels warn of this kind of blasphemy against the Holy Ghost saying:

> The Queen of the South shall rise up in judgement of the men of this generation, and condemn them: for she came from the uttermost parts of the earth to hear the wisdom of Solomon: and, behold, a greater than Solomon *is* here.

Here, the spirit of the Holy Ghost and the Queen of Sheba's passionate, questing, fiery spirit come together. The south wind is hot and dry. In Arabian alchemy the sublimation process is called the great south wind. Christian mystics equated it with the Holy Spirit which arms with the fire of love. The Queen of the South, Sheba, was seen by the alchemists to personify this quality of feminine wisdom. She is a questing spirit of truth, fired by love, very much an explorer at heart.

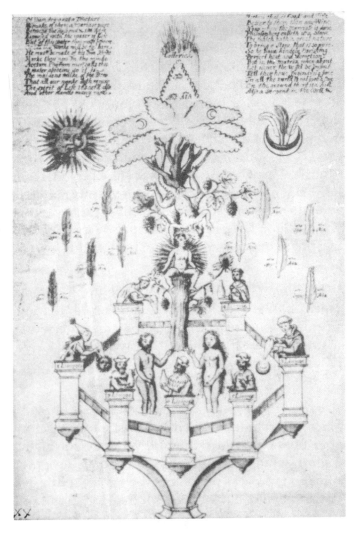

Figure 33. Melusina at the top of the Tree of Wisdom, with male and female at the base. (From the so-called Ripley Scrowle MS, 1588.)

Marie Louise von Franz, in her brilliant analysis of the Alchemical treatise *Aurora Consurgens*, draws together much of the imagery surrounding the Queen of Sheba, as wisdom and Aurora Dawn:

Who is she that looketh forth
as the morning, fair as the moon,
clear as the sun? (Song of Songs 6:9)

Aquinas in *Aurora Consurgens* says, "This is wisdom, namely the Queen of the South, who is said to have come from the East, like unto the morning rising."[3] Psychologically this means that the dawning of the day, before sunrise, one can feel or see, perhaps in a dream, she who is "fair as the moon, clear as the sun, *and* terrible as an army with banners." There is a desire to understand and terrible fear as well. The alchemists, typically practical, say that this work on oneself can begin at dawn, before sunrise, while there is still dew and before the Sun robs the Earth of its dew in order to nourish itself, and leaves the Earth "a widow and without husband." At this time, aurora, or dawn, means that "there is a growing awareness of the luminosity of the unconscious. It is not a concentrated light like the sun but rather a diffused glow on the horizon, i.e., on the threshold of consciousness." This feminine light of the unconscious brings illumination, gnosis, and the real-

---

[3]See Marie Louise von Franz: *Aurora Consurgens: A Document Attributed to Thomas Aquinas on the Problem of Opposites in Alchemy*, Bollingen Series LXXVII, Tr. by R. F. C. Hull and A. S. B. Glover (New York: Pantheon Books, 1966), p. 204.

Figure 34. The Wisdom as Virgin and Tree of Life. The shining white dove, the *sal sapientae* wherein lies the whole magistery of the work, is the pure, chaste, wise, and rich Queen of Sheba (Reusner, Pandora, Basel, 1588).

ization of the self. The alchemical text promises that if one does the psychological work of becoming conscious, integrating the projections of one's shadow onto others, and holding the opposites, one will be delivered of "all the infirmities of the night."[4] These are described as "evil odours and vapors which infect the mind."

Psychologically, these are the poisonous, soul destroying, unexamined, received ideas, collective opinions, and repressed contents that reign when the heart is closed to true experience and individual reality. Thus Sheba, Queen of the South, was fired by her need, desire, and love of wisdom to hear, see, and understand the wisdom of Solomon. Her wounded feminine stance needed the actual living experience of an encounter with the wise man to heal her, but having sought the experience, having followed her heart and having opened her heart, and trusted herself, she finds herself whole, in love with God, and held in the embrace of Wisdom. (See figure 34.)

By unifying the opposites—Sun, Moon, dark, light, dry, moist, man, woman, King and Queen, consciousness and unconsciousness—in a transconscious process of inner marriage and *coniunctio*, and truly experiencing this knowing connection, one becomes whole.

---

[4]See *Aurora Consurgens,* pp. 206, 207.

Epilogue

Although I had begun to think about Solomon and Sheba many years ago, I didn't actually begin to write this book until I had a dream that seemed to compel me forward and downward, and then, upward and backward in a swirling motion. It was a profound beginning of creation dream. An opening, a flood; I became sorely disoriented by what I saw and almost fell, but I was caught and drawn to merge. I struggled to remain separate and related, and began to journey through this new but ancient realm of Solomon and Sheba.

Years later, when the book was written, I dreamt that each of my hands was full of stuff—essential *materia*. I brought my two hands together at the level of my heart with the intention that each of the elements in each hand should seek out and marry its opposite in the other hand. Immediately a sphere formed, with colors swirling around the surface and throughout the center, demonstrating that the opposites had, indeed, married. As I looked, the sphere became a perfect little baby in my hands. I awoke with the realization: it is Christmas Day.

—BBK

Bibliography

The Holy Books that are the basic sources for the work are:

The Holy Scriptures according to the Masoretic Text (Hebrew and English), Volumes I and II. Jewish Publication Society, Philadelphia, 1955.

The Holy Bible containing the Old and New Testaments. The King James Version. Eyre and Spottiswoode Publishers, Ltd., London.

The Jerusalem Bible. Doubleday and Company, Inc., Garden City, New York, 1966.

The Queen of Sheba and Her Only Son Menyelek (I) being The Book of the Glory of the Kings (Kebra Nagast). Translated by Sir. E. A. Wallis Budge, The African Publication Society, London, 1932.

The Holy Qur'an (Arabic and English). Text, Translation and Commentary by Abdullah Yusuf Ali. Publication of Tahrike Tarsile Qur'an, Inc., New York, 1988.

The alchemical works are:

Aurora Consurgens: A Document attributed to Thomas Aquinas on the problem of opposites in alchemy. Edited, with a commentary by Marie-Louise von Franz. Bolligen, Pantheon Books, 1966. A companion work to:

Mysterium Coniunctionis. C. G. Jung, Bollingen, Princeton University Press, 1963.

The Qabalistic work is:

The Zohar. Five volumes, translated by Harry Sperling and Maurice Simon. New York: Rebecca Bennet Publications, nd; London, Socino Press, 1984.

The archaeological works are:

Qataban and Sheba. Wendell Phillips. Harcourt, Brace and Co., New York, 1955.

Solomon and Sheba. Ed. James B. Pritchard. Phaidon Press Ltd., London, 1974.

About the Author

Dr. Barbara Black Koltuv received her Ph.D. in clinical psychology from Columbia University in 1962. She holds a diploma in psychoanalysis from the post-doctoral program at New York University, as well as a diploma and certificate as a Jungian analyst from the C.G. Jung Institute of New York. Dr. Koltuv has been a practicing analyst for more than 25 years. She specializes in matters of love, sexuality, and relationships—on both the human and archetypal realm. She currently has a private practice in New York City. She is on the Board of Directors and a faculty member of the C.G. Jung Institute, where she is a training analyst and supervisor. She has traveled extensively in Mexico, Central and South America, Europe and North Africa and has spent a great deal of time in Jerusalem. She is the mother of a daughter and a son. Dr. Koltuv is the author of *Book of Lilith* and *Weaving Woman* both published by Nicolas-Hays. She resides in New York City and Woodstock, New York, and is currently at work on a new book.